De/Compositions

Some of the Many Books by W. D. Snodgrass

POETRY

Heart's Needle
After Experience
Remains
The Fuehrer Bunker: A Cycle of Poems-in-Progress
Selected Poems, 1957–1987
W. D.'s Midnight Carnival
The Death of Cock Robin
Each in His Season

PROSE

In Radical Pursuit
After-Images: Autobiographical Sketches

TRANSLATIONS

Gallows Songs
Selected Translations

De/Compositions

↻ *101 Good Poems Gone Wrong*

W. D. Snodgrass

Graywolf Press

SAINT PAUL, MINNESOTA

Publication of this volume is made possible in part by a grant provided by the
Minnesota State Arts Board through an appropriation by the Minnesota State
Legislature, and by a grant from the National Endowment for the Arts. Significant
support has also been provided by the Bush Foundation; Dayton's Project Imagine
with support from Target Foundation; the McKnight Foundation; a grant made on
behalf of the Stargazer Foundation; and other generous contributions from founda-
tions, corporations, and individuals. To these organizations and individuals we offer
our heartfelt thanks.

Published by Graywolf Press
2402 University Avenue, Suite 203
Saint Paul, Minnesota 55114
All rights reserved.

www.graywolfpress.org

Published in the United States of America

ISBN 1-55597-317-5

2 4 6 8 9 7 5 3 1
First Graywolf Printing, 2001

Library of Congress Catalog Number: 00-105070

Cover design: Scott Sorenson

Acknowledgments

We gratefully acknowledge the cooperation of publishers, agents, and the authors for their permission to reprint the following works. In some cases, all best efforts were made on the author's behalf to gain permission to reprint.

"Musée des Beaux Arts," "Seen When Nights Are Young," and "Song of the Old Soldier" from *W. H. Auden: Collected Poems* by W. H. Auden. Copyright © 1976 by Edward Mendelson, William Meredith and Monroe K. Spears, Executors of the Estate of W. H. Auden. Used by permission of Random House, Inc.

#22, " 'Of 1826'" and #29 " 'There sat down, once'" from *The Dream Songs* by John Berryman. Copyright © 1969 by John Berryman. Copyright renewed 1997 by Kate Donahue Berryman. Reprinted by permission of Farrar, Straus and Giroux, LLC.

"The Fish" from *The Complete Poems 1927–1979* by Elizabeth Bishop. Copyright © 1979, 1983 by Alice Helen Methfessel. Reprinted by permission of Farrar, Straus and Giroux, LLC.

"At Melville's Tomb" and "Repose of Rivers" from *Complete Poems of Hart Crane* by Hart Crane, edited by Marc Simon. Copyright 1933, © 1958, 1966 by Liveright Publishing Corporation. Copyright © 1986 by Marc Simon. Used by permission of Liveright Publishing Corporation.

"I Know a Man" by Robert Creeley © 1983 by the Regents of the University of California. Reprinted from *Collected Poems of Robert Creeley, 1945–1975* with the permission of the University of California Press.

Contents

III. The Singular Voice

IV. Metrics & Music

for
Kathy:

right, at last

The De/Composer

One of my favorite stanzas in the English language comes from Thomas Hardy's "Transformations." An old man walks musing in a familiar graveyard.

> These grasses must be made
> Of her who often prayed,
> Last century, for repose;
> And the fair girl long ago
> Whom I vainly tried to know
> May be entering this rose.

The stanza below comes from the poem de/composed by W. D. Snodgrass, with his de/composed title, "Resurrections":

> These grasses must be she
> Who prayed, last century,
> For peace, after life's woes;
> And the girl, fair and sweet,
> I had often tried to meet
> Is reborn in this rose.

It's hilarious. (See the whole poems on pages 64–65.) Many of Snodgrass's de/compositions are comic—and when they are not comic they remain instructive. These de/compositions are not parody, which ties idiosyncrasies of style to inappropriate subject matter. Snodgrass has invented a way to show the minute, yet gross differences that separate good poetry from terrible poetry. He isolates good poetry by setting it next to bad, and demonstrates that the poem is not its paraphrase even when the paraphrase follows the shape and syntax of the real poem. Sometimes he achieves a similar effect by printing a poet's finished poem beside a poet's earlier draft.

Critics have proclaimed forever that the paraphrase of a poem is not the poem. (Then they proceed to violate their truism.) The poem is the whole of the poem, and nothing but the poem. It is vowels and metaphors; it is almost-invisible connections by the associations of words; it is paradox and contradiction that derive from the connotations of whole words—and not from what a dictionary or a thesaurus call synonyms.

I speak of almost-invisible connections. The underside of a poem provides an aesthetic wholeness that may have nothing to do with a reasonable paraphrase. In "Transformations," there are several such connections, one of which I have never seen mentioned. In the underside of the poem, Hardy makes transsexual images. In the first stanza the male is "bosomed" at the yew tree's foot, while his wife may become a "shoot." When the fair girl—"know" carries sexual inference—is pictured as "entering" the flower, she is granted a verb associated with male penetration. I do not suggest that Hardy intended this connection, but these images make part of an internal order that we absorb even when we have no notion that we are absorbing it. Order makes coherence. Of course the de/composed version shows no aesthetic wholeness whatsoever.

Over the years, I have read with delight the de/compositions as De composed them (De/compositions indeed) with a growing wonder at his resourcefulness in matching and maiming at the same time. Of course, I am grateful to be included, even if I perpetrated the de/composition myself, in my original version of "The Man in the Dead Machine." Thank heaven one is permitted (or I permit myself) to believe that my poem is *my* poem, and that I have the right or duty to re/compose, even a decade or so later.

Welcome to a book of poems, half of which are terrible, a book that again and again isolates the qualities of true poetry. Poetry is what gets lost in de/composition.

Donald Hall

Introduction

During the 1930s, the British poet and critic William Empson was teaching English Renaissance Literature at a commune school in China. When the Japanese invaded in 1937, the whole school, teachers and students together, fled on foot, hiking over the mountains and holding classes as they went. Empson, noted for a prodigious memory, had no textbook with him and so taught his classes, including the texts, from memory. When he came to John Donne—with whose work he was slightly less familiar than, say, that of Milton—he occasionally had trouble recalling Donne's text and, here and there, made up a word or two, even a line, to fill out the original. After some weeks, he noticed that one of the boys at the back of the group was busy writing and went back to see why. To his astonishment, he found the boy had brought his own book and was cancelling passages of the original to write in Empson's improvisations.

Empson sometimes told this story on himself; we will probably never know whether he then provided the class with corrections of the "de/compositions" he and his student had jointly produced, much less whether he discussed the relative merits of Donne's version against his own. I suspect that if Empson forgot any part of a fine poem that would be one of the least crucial, least meaningful elements.

Just the opposite, when I taught the reading or speaking of poems, I often found the best way to do that was to deliberately alter the most memorable, most crucial aspects. After reading the poem aloud to fix it in the class's hearing, I'd get a student to read with me. Since the de/compositions usually match line by line, he or she would read a line of the original; I'd follow with my *ersatz* version. When we'd finished, I'd ask what was the most scandalous thing I'd done to the poem. The natural urge to find one's teacher wrong usually provoked lively exchanges, bringing the students into close contact with the true text. With a little nudging, this could reveal how local excellences interconnected to form a basic structure. Often, my "direction" of the class lay only in a half-joking defense of my version or in an attack on some aspect of the original, meant to rally their support and grasp of that text.

Not infrequently, one of my students claimed to prefer the de/composed version. It was sometimes hard not to answer this, but instead to let the discussion disperse it. Students with nerve enough to say what they really thought (not what they thought I wanted to hear) are too great an asset to be embarrassed or intimidated. Often enough, those "dead wrong" students would go on to make startling leaps, working toward their own discoveries, not waiting to hear what was "right." Besides, learning to change one's mind may be half an education.

While putting this collection together, I found that my de/compositions fell naturally into five sections according to the particular excellence I was trying to dissolve or drive out. Not surprisingly, this proved to be related to the ways that the language of poems tends to differ from that of instructions, arguments, or prose discourse generally:

    I.   Abstract & General vs. Concrete & Specific
   II.   Undercurrents
  III.   The Singular Voice
  IV.   Metrics & Music
   V.   Structure & Climax

The first section deals with a problem particularly troublesome to my students, many of whom were young poets. When we discuss poems, we quite properly tend toward abstract terms: freedom, love, humanity, etc. This might suggest that the poem's business is to offer summations and solutions, to present a generally applicable "message." Such interpretative terms are indeed a part, but only a part, of the minds we aim to record.

My second section deals with the way that a poem's meaning often lies beneath its prose or "dictionary" sense; since it is found in implication and suggestion, so demanding sensitive interpretation. The third section acknowledges that a poet's voice may convey a recognizable identity, though this may or may not relate directly to the author's known or supposed qualities. In any case, the more familiar we are with the work of a particular poet, the more meaning we are likely to derive from his/her individual works.

The fourth section continues the pursuit of significance and intensity below the poem's conscious surface into its music and rhythm. Obviously, we derive some kinds of meaning from the movement and music of language, although this may lie in areas of emotion and impulsion well beneath our conscious and intellectual awareness. The fifth and final section investigates how words and phrases nourish and enrich each other, so building the poem's shape and structure.

Although the book's sections are defined by these qualities, it has often proven impossible to impair one effect without affecting others as well. In the Commentary at the end of each section, I've suggested how I see the relation between each poem and its de/composition. This is intended only to suggest a useful jumping-off point in the unlikely event that none suggests itself; it does not mean to conclude discussion or to give any final or exclusive interpretation. Dealing with something so rich and strange as a poem, there is no guarantee (not even, perhaps, a desirability) that different readers find identical answers. Poems are not only produced by individual sensibilities; they are also received and interpreted by individuals. The better the poem, the more likely it is not only to carry its "maker's mark" but also to accept a multiplicity of readings. There *do* seem to be times when we can agree that a specific interpretation is merely wrong; the number of right readings may be limited only by the number of possible readers.

Often, my de/compositions are easier to understand than the originals—usually because there is less to understand in them. It is also easier to tie up an animal whose blood has been drained; creatures not subject to taxidermy are less easily corralled, more likely to yield surprises both pleasant and shocking. Many of the de/compositions render a poem's denotative or dictionary sense while stripping away connotations, suggestions, the inflections of living beings. Without the intuitive, less conscious, and intellectual elements, this de/composed "literal" or "surface" meaning often yields roughly what you'd get if the poem were translated into a second language, then translated back. For a reader with an inquiring mind—not too ready to take answers where questions are still possible—the poem may offer opportunities for lifelong discoveries.

I have not always resisted the temptation to make my versions comical. As W. H. Auden noted, there are few things funnier than bad poems. Athletes, watching a film of a past game or race, no doubt laugh at their opponents' blunders—even at their own. Works of art, however, have an added problem: the rules always change because no two situations are the same. What we learn about one poem may yield no general principle for others (including any poems that the students may be writing). Just so, chess players study the games of the masters even though that exact situation will probably never exist again for them to face. Instead we are trying to learn how one mind faced a particular situation, and perhaps to temper our own minds toward others' possibilities. In any case, the deliberate failures of my versions, even when amusing, should not distract anyone from the real subject: the abiding successes of the real poems.

I am laying out a game, then, that provokes readers (alone or in a group) to ask what makes fine poems fine. Enriching our responses can be a long process but that may be one of the best things about it. You can't get rich quick; the chance to get rich gradually—perhaps lifelong—may be worth more.

I

Abstract & General
vs.
Concrete & Specific

Leda and the Swan

—William Butler Yeats

A sudden blow: the great wings beating still
Above the staggering girl, her thighs caressed
By the dark webs, her nape caught in his bill,
He holds her helpless breast upon his breast.

How can those terrified vague fingers push
The feathered glory from her loosening thighs?
And how can body, laid in that white rush,
But feel the strange heart beating where it lies?

A shudder in the loins engenders there
The broken wall, the burning roof and tower
And Agamemnon dead.[1]
                      Being so caught up,
So mastered by the brute blood of the air,
Did she put on his knowledge with his power
Before the indifferent beak could let her drop?

↻ Leda and the Swan

—de/composed from Yeats

An unforseen assault; that huge form still
Above the helpless girl, dazed and distressed
By the attack, then pinned down by his will
And massive force, powerless and oppressed.

---

[1] Events of the Trojan War and its aftermath.

How shall her terror-stricken throes escape
Immortal radiance o'erwhelming her;
And how can she, benumbed still with that rape,
Not feel the deity, inside her, stir?

Divine insemination commences there
The rise of Western empires, fall of Troy
And Eastern culture dead. Being caught up so,
Subjected to the iron will of the air,
Did she, too, see our future, share the joy
Zeus felt, before his wings could let her go?

Leda and the Swan

      —Yeats's first version from *Tomorrow* (Dublin)
        (italicized passages revised in the later version)

A rush, a sudden wheel, and hovering still
The bird descends, and her frail thighs are pressed
By the *webbed toes, and that all-powerful* bill
Has laid her helpless *face* upon his breast.
How can those terrified vague fingers push
The feathered glory from her loosening thighs!
All the stretched body's laid on the white rush
And feels the strange heart beating where it lies.
A shudder in the loins engenders there
The broken wall, the burning roof and tower,
And Agamemnon dead.
                 Being so caught up,
So mastered by the brute blood of the air,
Did she put on his knowledge with his power
Before the indifferent beak could let her drop?

Dream Song #22, "Of 1826"

—John Berryman

I am the little man who smokes & smokes.
I am the girl who does know better but.
I am the king of the pool.
I am so wise I had my mouth sewn shut.
I am a government official & a goddamned fool.
I am a lady who takes jokes.

I am the enemy of the mind.
I am the auto salesman and lóve you.
I am a teenage cancer, with a plan.
I am the blackt-out man.
I am the woman powerful as a zoo.
I am two eyes screwed to my set, whose blind—

It is the Fourth of July.
Collect: while the dying man[1]
forgone by you creator, who forgives,
is gasping "Thomas Jefferson still lives"
in vain, in vain, in vain.
I am Henry Pussy-cat! My whiskers fly.

---

[1] John Adams who, like Thomas Jefferson, died on the 50th anniversary of the signing of
the Declaration of Independence.

↻ Of American History

—de/composed from Berryman

I am an ordinary man with unhealthy addictions.
I am a young woman who does things against her conscience.
I have absolute power over those around me.
I am too clever to speak out on controversial issues.
I obtained high status without ability.
I am a noblewoman who tolerates indignities.

I am opposed to free thought.
I will pretend affection to get your money.
I am a progressive malignancy intent on taking power.
I am an empty personality.
I am a female full of caged bestiality.
I watch nothing but commercial entertainments.

This is our nation's 50th anniversary.
Join in; while John Adams, dying—
our founding father who forgives our lapses from our values—
is gasping "Thomas Jefferson still lives"
though Jefferson lay dying that same day,
I am a lecherous young man who delights in all this corruption.

Disillusionment of Ten O'Clock

—Wallace Stevens

The houses are haunted
By white night-gowns.
None are green,
Or purple with green rings,
Or green with yellow rings,
Or yellow with blue rings.
None of them are strange,
With socks of lace
And beaded ceintures.
People are not going
To dream of baboons and periwinkles.
Only, here and there, an old sailor,
Drunk and asleep in his boots,
Catches tigers
In red weather.

Complaint at Nightfall

—de/composed from Stevens

The houses are haunted
By colorless nightwear.
None have lively colors,
Or gaudy decorations,
Clashing vividly
And daringly vulgar.
None of them are strange,
With extravagant features
Or exotic trimmings.
People are not going
To dream of brute beasts or tiny beauties.
Only, here and there, an old man,
Drunk and asleep in his work clothes,
Dreams of adventures
In dangerous times.

Globe

—Elizabeth Spires

I spread my game on the cracked linoleum floor:
I had to play inside all day.
The woman who kept me said so.
She was middle-aged, drank tea in the middle of the day,
her face the color of dust layered on a table.

A high window let in alley light
to a two-room apartment.
Sofas and chairs bristled like hedgehogs
and made the back of my legs itch.
No red flowers on the windowsill. No radio.
Just waxy vines drooping over the tables,
a dome clock dividing time into fifteen-minute parcels.

What did I do all day?
Made card houses so frail
I had to turn my breath the other way.
Or colored the newspaper comic strips,
or wobbled across the floor in my mother's old pumps
with the aplomb of somebody drunk.

Enter my father at 5:15, dark and immediate,
finished with his shift at the factory.
He was hiding something behind his back.
He turned as I circled him,
keeping whatever it was out of sight.
Close your eyes and hold out your hand—
I touched a globe slotted on top for coins,
my hand shadowing the continents

My Father's Values in the World

—de/composed from Spires

My childhood was lonely and cursed by poverty.
I was depressed by confinement and lack of freedom
caused by the absence of parental care in the home
which relegated me to the care of unfamiliar substitute-parents,
especially one old lady who was a real sourpuss.

Our home situation was dingy
And constricted.
The furnishings were uncomfortable
which made me feel irritated.
We had no small luxuries which could light up your life.
The only beauty-touches were some dumb plants
and a fancy centerpiece from our affluent period.

Consequently I passed my time
Feeling that people's lives were insecure
and subject to threat from the smallest things.
I sought pleasure in cheap, popular entertainments.
I tried prematurely to assume adult roles but my amusements
displayed my anxiety that adults were unstable and untrustworthy.

I felt differently about my father, though; I really loved him so much.
He was stern but hard working and reliable.
Besides, sometimes he brought me presents.
My life literally revolved around him.
I never knew what he had in store for me
but I felt I could trust him blindly.
He just gave me the whole world.

Globe (continued)

like a cloud thousands of miles wide.
He put my finger over the state where we lived,
then handed me his loose change to fill the world up with.

Memory's false as anything, spliced in the wrong parts,
queerly jumping. But better than forgetting.
We walked out into the soft light of October, leaves
sticking to our shoes like gold paper.
I was four years old and he was twenty-five,
same age as I am writing this.

In his presence, my consciousness opened up
and became so expansive
since he taught me the meaning of Life and how we relate to others.
Also the value of saving money. His generosity just filled my soul.

That's the way it really was. Honest.
So let's not forget our loving parents.
He introduced me to conditions outside our domestic life
and transformed all existence into something valuable and honored.
Now I've grown up, too,
and learned my lessons from him.

The Fury of Aerial Bombardment

—Richard Eberhart

You would think the fury of aerial bombardment
Would rouse God to relent; the infinite spaces
Are still silent. He looks on shock-pried faces.
History, even, does not know what is meant.

You would feel that after so many centuries
God would give man to repent; yet he can kill
As Cain could, but with multitudinous will,
No farther advanced than in his ancient furies.

Was man made stupid to see his own stupidity?
Is God by definition indifferent, beyond us all?
Is the eternal truth man's fighting soul
Wherein the Beast ravens in its own avidity?

Of Van Wettering I speak, and Averill,
Names on a list, whose faces I do not recall
But they are gone to early death, who late in school
Distinguished the belt feed lever from the belt holding pawl.[1]

---

[1] Parts of a machine gun.

Artillery and Aerial Bombardments

—de/composed from Eberhart

You'd think artillery and aerial bombardments
Would bring the Lord to stop all wars. Yet God
Says nothing. Men just stare upward open-jawed.
Not even wise men think that this makes sense.

You would feel that after so many ages
Men would decide to quit; yet they can kill
As Cain could, but with whole nations' will,
Like savages in their hunger and old rages.

What purpose can be served by mankind's stupidity?
Is God content whatever happens to us all?
Is the real truth that somewhere in Man's soul
We wallow in Satan's greed and fierce cupidity?

I think of the young soldiers at their roll call,
Names on a list whose faces I will never see
For they've been slaughtered, one and all,
Who'd newly learned the use of weaponry.

Further de/composed final stanza:

Now let's remember those who fought by our side;
So they'll not die in vain, we must recall
How they gave up their lives to save us all
And further that great cause for which they died.

The Groundhog

—Richard Eberhart

In June, amid the golden fields,
I saw a groundhog lying dead.
Dead lay he; my senses shook,
And mind outshot our naked frailty.
There lowly in the vigorous summer
His form began its senseless change,
And made my senses waver dim
Seeing nature ferocious in him.
Inspecting close his maggots' might
And seething cauldron of his being,
Half with loathing, half with a strange love,
I poked him with an angry stick.
The fever arose, became a flame
And Vigour circumscribed the skies,
Immense energy in the sun,
And through my frame a sunless trembling.
My stick had done nor good nor harm.
Then stood I silent in the day
Watching the object, as before;
And kept my reverence for knowledge
Trying for control, to be still,
To quell the passion in the blood;
Until I had bent down on my knees
Praying for joy in the sight of decay.
And so I left; and I returned
In Autumn strict of eye, to see
The sap gone out of the groundhog,
But the bony sodden hulk remained.
But the year had lost its meaning,

A De/Composing Animal

—de/composed from Eberhart

In early summer in the fields
I saw an animal lying dead.
He didn't move; my senses shook—
My mind fled Man's mortality.
On the ground in the flourishing summer
His form began its meaningless change,
Making me draw my senses back
Seeing nature operate in him.
Noting how small insects moved
In the active decay of his corpse,
And filled with conflicting emotions,
I disturbed him with a sharp stick.
The turmoil grew stronger, began to burn,
And Growth defined the universe,
Immense energy was everywhere
But a deadening fear grew in my soul.
My act had had no real effect.
Then I stood silent in the field
Watching the creature as before,
And put my faith and trust in the mind,
Trying to control myself, keep calm,
Not give in to the physical
Until I had made a prayer to be
Affirmative in spite of change.
And so I left; I looked again
Months later with keen eyes, to see
The creature's vital juices gone
But the dead body was still there.
Yet the march of time had lost its meaning

And in intellectual chains
I lost both love and loathing,
Mured up in the wall of wisdom.
Another summer took the fields again
Massive and burning, full of life,
But when I chanced upon the spot
There was only a little hair left,
And bones bleaching in the sunlight
Beautiful as architecture;
I watched like a geometer,
And cut a walking stick from a birch.
It has been three years, now.
There is no sign of the groundhog.
I stood there in the whirling summer,
My hand capped a withered heart,
And thought of China and of Greece,
Of Alexander in his tent;
Of Montaigne in his tower,
Of Saint Theresa in her wild lament.

A De/Composing Animal (continued)

And, bound up in my own theories,
I lost all strong emotions,
Sealed off in my own ideas.
Summer came to the field again
With universal intensity
But when I came back to the spot
Only a few remains were left
And the skeleton there in plain sight
Showed the animal's inner structure;
I watched like a philosopher
Preparing myself for life's journey.
It has been a long time now
There is nothing left of the animal.
Humbled there in busy summer,
Shielding my frightened, withdrawn heart.
I thought of civilizations gone,
Of heroes whose great lives were spent,
Of Mankind's greatest thinkers lost
Then made for all mankind this sad lament.

Still to Be Neat

—Ben Jonson

Still[1] to be neat, still to be dressed,
As you were going to a feast;
Still to be powdered, still perfumed:
Lady, it is to be presumed,
Though art's hid causes are not found,
All is not sweet, all is not sound.

Give me a look, give me a face
That makes simplicity a grace;
Robes loosely flowing, hair as free:
Such sweet neglect more taketh me
Than all th' adulteries of art;
They strike mine eyes, but not my heart.

[1]Always.

Always Decked Out

—de/composed from Jonson

Always decked out in the height of fashion
As if dressed for some grand occasion;
Face made up, smartly turned out—
Lady, you give us cause for doubt:
Why you've dressed up may not be clear
But things don't all seem wholesome here.

I like an aspect and lineaments
With plainness for their ornaments;
Clothing loose, hair without fetter:
I find such simple ways much better
Than all the flirtatious charms of art;
Their glamour never strikes my heart.

Sonnet #129

—William Shakespeare

The expense[1] of spirit in a waste of shame
Is lust in action; and till action, lust
Is perjured, murderous, bloody, full of blame,
Savage, extreme, rude, cruel, not to trust,
Enjoyed[2] no sooner but despiséd straight,
Past reason hunted; and no sooner had,
Past reason hated, as a swallowed bait
On purpose laid to make the taker mad:
Mad in pursuit, and in possession so;
Had, having, and in quest to have, extreme;
A bliss in proof,[3] and proved, a very woe;
Before, a joy proposed; behind, a dream.
    All this the world well knows; yet none knows well
    To shun the heaven that leads men to this hell.

↻ Sonnet #129

—de/composed from Shakespeare, A

Vigor and spunk drain out to barren guilt
In casual sex. To bring it off, we lie,
Accuse, cheat, kill; first tears are spilt,
Then blood; we slash, stab, gouge out groin or eye.
Once she's been laid, she's like some loathsome bug;

---

[1] Loss.
[2] Sexually possessed.
[3] When tried.

She's been too long pursued—once she's been had,
She's too much hated, like some secret drug
Slipped into someone's drink to make him mad.
It's mad pursuing her, mad once she's captured;
Laid, laying, schemes to lay her—all insane.
Your long-sought Eden sours when you've trapped her.
Before, dreams of bliss; after, dead dreams' pain.
　　　All this the world knows since we've warned them well
　　　To seek some other pleasure than this hell.

↻ Sonnet #129

　　　　　—de/composed from Shakespeare, B

In casual sex, we jeopardize our souls
And all their powers. Seeking intercourse,
We take wrong means to reach illicit goals,
Behaving lawlessly with undue force.
When they're achieved, such pleasures are despised.
They're sought past reason and if brought about
Are too much hated—like a plot devised
So all sound judgement would be driven out—
Frenzied in the seeking and the act;
Before, throughout and after, too extreme;
A joy to try out, but a grief in fact;
A bliss imagined, then a shattered dream.
　　　All men have heard this yet none seems to know
　　　That seeking such joys only leads to woe.

A Noiseless Patient Spider

—Walt Whitman, 1868

A noiseless patient spider,
I mark'd where on a little promontory it stood isolated;
Mark'd how to explore the vacant vast surrounding,
It launch'd forth filament, filament, filament, out of itself;
Ever unreeling them, ever tirelessly speeding them.

And you O my Soul where you stand,
Surrounded, detached, in measureless oceans of space,
Ceaselessly musing, venturing, throwing, seeking the spheres, to connect them;
Till the bridge you will need be form'd, till the ductile anchor hold;
Till the gossamer thread you fling catch somewhere, O my Soul.

The Soul, Reaching, Throwing Out for Love

—Whitman's first version, ca. 1862

The Soul, reaching, throwing out for love,
As the spider, from some little promontory, throwing out filament after
    filament, tirelessly out of itself, that one at least may catch and form a
    link, a bridge, a connection
O I saw one passing along, saying hardly a word—yet full of love I detected
    him, by certain signs
O eyes wishfully turning! O silent eyes!
For then I thought of you o'er the world,
O latent oceans, fathomless oceans of love!
O waiting oceans of love! yearning and fervid! and of you sweet souls
    perhaps in the future, delicious and long:
But Death, unknown on the earth—ungiven, dark here, unspoken, never born:
You fathomless latent souls of love—you pent and unknown oceans of love!

The Man in the Dead Machine

—Donald Hall, first version

High on a slope in New Guinea
the Grumman Hellcat[1]
lodges among bright vines
as thick as arms. In 1942,
the clenched hand of a pilot
glided it here
where no one has ever been.

In the cockpit the helmeted
skeleton sits
upright, held
by dry sinews at neck
and shoulder, and webbing
that straps the pelvic cross
to the cracked
leather of the seat, and the breastbone
to the canvas cover
of the parachute.

Or say that the shrapnel
missed him, he flew
back to the carrier, and every
morning takes his chair, his pale
hands on the black arms, and sits
upright, held
by the firm webbing.

---

[1]U.S. fighter plane, World War II.

The Man in the Dead Machine

—Hall's revisions in italics

High on a slope in New Guinea
the Grumman Hellcat
lodges among bright vines
as thick as arms. In *nineteen-forty-three,*
the clenched hand of a pilot
glided it here
where no one has ever been.

In the cockpit the helmeted
skeleton sits
upright, held
by dry sinews at neck
and shoulder, and by webbing
that straps the pelvic cross
to the cracked
leather of the seat, and the breastbone
to the canvas cover
of the parachute.

Or say that the shrapnel
missed *me, I* flew
back to the carrier and every morning
take the train, *my* pale
hands on *a black case,* and *sit*
upright, held
by the firm webbing.

I Know a Man

—Robert Creeley

As I sd to my
friend, because I am
always talking,—John, I

sd, which was not his
name, the darkness sur-
rounds us, what

can we do against
it, or else, shall we &
why not, buy a goddamn big car,

drive, he sd, for
christ's sake, look
out where yr going.

For the Future's Sake

—de/composed from Creeley

I said to my friend—
we always discuss this—
"John," I said to him

(that's not his real name)
"evils are universal;
what can we do

to ameliorate suffering
or should we just get
more luxurious comforts?"

"For the future's sake" he answered,
"consider the possible
harm to the ecology."

Eros Turannos

—Edwin Arlington Robinson

She fears him, and will always ask
    What fated her to choose him;
She meets in his engaging mask
    All reasons to refuse him;
But what she meets and what she fears
Are less than are the downward years,
Drawn slowly to the foamless weirs
    Of age, were she to lose him.

Between a blurred sagacity
    That once had powers to sound him,
And Love, that will not let him be
    The Judas that she found him,
Her pride assuages her almost,
As if it were alone the cost.
He sees that he will not be lost,
    And waits and looks around him.

A sense of ocean and old trees
    Envelops and allures him;
Tradition, touching all he sees,
    Beguiles and reassures him;
And all her doubts of what he says
Are dimmed by what she knows of days—
Till even prejudice delays
    And fades, and she secures him.

The falling leaf inaugurates
    The reign of her confusion:

↻ Love, the Tyrant

—de/composed from Robinson

She fears him, and has always been
    Amazed that she should choose him;
She meets in his engaging grin
    All reasons to refuse him;
But the sharp avarice she fears
Is better than the lonely years
Of spinsterhood or all the sneers
    Of neighbors, should she lose him.

Between a blurred sagacity
    That once had power to sound him,
And Love, denying he could be
    The Don Juan that she found him,
Her pride assuages her almost
As if that were the worst she's lost.
He sighs while reckoning up the cost
    Of her fine goods around him.

A sense of luxury and ease
    Envelops and allures him;
Old money, touching all he sees,
    Beguiles and reassures him;
And her doubts that he tells the truth
Are less than are her fading youth;
And though her friends find him uncouth
    She marries and secures him.

His late nights out inaugurate
    The reign of her confusion

The pounding wave reverberates
    The dirge of her illusion;
And home, where passion lived and died,
Becomes a place where she can hide,
While all the town and harbor side
    Vibrate with her seclusion.

We tell you, tapping on our brows,
    The story as it should be,
As if the story of a house
    Were told, or ever could be;
We'll have no kindly veil between
Her visions and those we have seen,
As if we guessed what hers have been,
    Or what they are or would be.

Meanwhile we do no harm; for they
    That with a god have striven,
Not hearing much of what we say,
    Take what the god has given;
Though like waves breaking it may be,
Or like a changed familiar tree,
Or like a stairway to the sea
    Where down the blind are driven.

Love, the Tyrant (continued)

While gossips' tongues reverberate
    The dirge of her illusion;
And home, where she lived out her dreams
Falls into ruin through his schemes
Till all the town and harbor seems
    To know their love's conclusion.

I tell you, tapping on my brows
    The story true and rightful—
That those who gamble and carouse
    Soon find a fate that's frightful:
In their great house, dark as the tomb,
He sleeps now in a separate room
Or, seeking girls of fresher bloom,
    Prowls the dark streets at nightfall.

Meanwhile, I do no harm for they
    Who by their love are driven,
Not hearing much of what I say,
    Take what their love has given;
Though it be like storm winds deranged,
Or like familiar landscapes changed,
Or to live bitter and estranged
    Together, unforgiven.

I. Abstract & General vs. Concrete & Specific

Most teachers and handbooks of creative writing advise students to present, not to tell—to give an experience rather than an interpretation of events or persons that the reader or listener has not encountered. Although things aren't quite so simple, that is often good advice. To be valued for long, a poem must offer something new, not found elsewhere, an element of invention and surprise. William Wordsworth noted how hard it was "to give to universally received truths a pathos and spirit which shall readmit them into the soul like revelations of the moment." As this implies, most general ideas and abstractions have been around a long time; even if *we* have newly discovered them, others may find them less than captivating. Without the spice—or more aptly, the meat—of particular fact and/or personal voice as the benchmark of an individual mind, they remain familiar and "used."

This section's poems, by widely differing poets, are composed largely of vivid, concrete details that I have replaced, in the de/compositions, with abstractions, changing personal speech into committee diction; later in this section, my versions explore other ways general ideas may become personal.

It's reported that when W. B. Yeats asked his secretary to copy "Leda and the Swan," she threw up her hands and resigned. No living typist would lose an hour's pay on reading my version; the loss of physical details and actions—specific nouns and verbs displaced by interpretative adjectives—drives out Yeats's immediacy. We share neither Leda's bewilderment at the brutal rape nor her bafflement about the far-flung consequences that are part of Zeus's intention: the Trojan War and the rise of Western culture over that of Troy and the East. Yeats's revisions after his first published version show clearly his desire to heighten that jolting experience. Further, I have omitted Yeats's one emotionally interpretative word, "indifferent," which carries a strong shock after our more physical encounter with Leda's ravishment.

John Berryman's "Dream Song #22" uses a sophisticatedly kooky language to depict our vast carnival of faults and failings. The speaker's delight in listing these stereotypes should, perhaps, warn and prepare us for his climactic switch from scorn to boastful membership and an implied invitation: "Come on in; the corruption's fine!"

In contrast, Wallace Stevens's "Disillusionment of Ten O'Clock" laments our lack of risk and variety (the very qualities Berryman alternately scorns and celebrates) but does so with all the verve and color that it claims is lacking.

Elizabeth Spires's "Globe" addresses a more private and personal subject—the moving portrayal of a hard-working and defining father. The de/composition not only obliterates the facts and details of the speaker's experience, but also her recreation of the child's language—my vague and general terminology has an air of highbrow pretension. This, in turn, undermines the poem's climax: the switch into an adult's voice questioning her memory's reliability. My version simply commands the reader: "I had a rough time; now feel sad about that!"

As noted, though, this question is not entirely one-sided. True, sense impressions *do* demand our attention—they protect our lives from dangers around us. Yet our beliefs and opinions help to shape whatever lives we save, may even lead us to risk those lives defending our theories. We cannot honestly discuss or represent our lives, any more than our poems, without using ideational language.

In "The Fury of Aerial Bombardment," Richard Eberhart reverses our usual practice of first noting details and facts, then deriving from them an abstract or general conclusion. After three stanzas of broad speculation, rather like many editorials, speeches, or bad poems, we leap to a climax of sharp, personal details. A terrible irony emerges: our memory of war retains the roll call of fellow trainees and the names of machine-gun parts; the faces are irrevocably lost. "The Groundhog" returns to the more common organization: after each revisit to the animal's decomposing body, the speaker speculates further on life's duration and meaning. In the climactic close, however, he turns again to specific examples very much his own, personal and unpredictable.

Despite such details as "powdered" and "perfumed," the language of Ben Jonson's "Still to Be Neat" seems fairly general: to speak of being "neat" or of making "simplicity a grace" is scarcely specific. Elsewhere, however, we are caught by a characterizing liveliness of voice: "sweet neglect" or "th' adulteries of art" are, sadly, not the sort of language we hear every day.

William Shakespeare's "Sonnet #129" is built almost entirely of generalizations; it will surprise no one that my de/composition A, offering specific details and acts, is immeasurably poorer. De/composition B, even more abstract than the original, assumes that the "message content" or "moral," though actually something we hear all our lives—one of Wordsworth's "universally received truths"—is of crucial interest. Here again, the rendering of personality through the individual voice is essential. Heard alone, Shakespeare's first line might seem a riddle—as if he'd devised an obscure, private language for this common problem. Further surprise lies in the elegantly balanced structure of opposites—line against line, half-line against half-line. Many feel that a subject so violent requires a similar style, yet our minds are not quite so simple. Conflict—here, the clash of subject matter and treatment—still informs our condition. We do not lack orderly discourse about our fiercer instincts, only the ability to control them. The furious tone, the powerful echoes of word, phrase, and sound, render a highly conflicted individual who passionately denounces passion.

The two versions of Walt Whitman's "A Noiseless Patient Spider" raise the related problem of the personal and the universal. The canceled first version is much more specific about the application of the spider's action—the finding of a lover or friend. In the revision, the spider's acts are presented in greater detail, but their application is more readily universal—a reaching out to all aspects of experience.

The two versions of Donald Hall's "The Man in the Dead Machine" might seem to move in the opposite direction. The earlier version depicts a wartime casualty and makes what seems a general application: "Why has our society bound and deadened us, the survivors?" With the change from the third- to the first-person, the same details raise a sharper, more personal dilemma: "Why have I chosen this kind of life?" This question—which most of us ask at some time—makes the poem simultaneously more personal and more universal.

In Robert Creeley's "I Know a Man," the eccentric style—abbreviations, fragmented sentences, conflicts between syntax and line breaks—forces a reader to attend closely to details, just as the speaker's friend says he should do. Style is, in large part, the subject—the speaker's mockery of himself as a man so filled with grand ideas that he drives dangerously and may even be unsure who he's talking to. (While the present book was in manuscript, I accidentally altered the poem's first word from "As" to "And"—a telling example of the loss probable from even the smallest change in a fine poem. "As" implies "For instance" while "And" means only "Next"—the de/composition's omission of both suggests that the interest lies in an impersonal report of an event.)

Edwin Arlington Robinson's splendid "Eros Turannos" shies away from specific details—we do not even know whether the central couple are married or how "he" betrayed "her." The grubby (and drearily expectable) facts of my de/composition certainly offer no improvement, meanwhile adding a trite and obvious moral in stanza V. In the original, however, the townspeople's choral voice is sharply characterized by constantly developing images drawn from nature, so implying that such betrayals are simply part of the landscape and of life's weather. Even more vocally defining is Robinson's virtuoso rhyme scheme; the de/composition maintains these patterns, but dissolves their sense of constantly swelling tensions and releasings.

• • •

"No ideas but in things," said William Carlos Williams, so defining for many of his generation their revolt against the high-flown sentiments and ideational language of earlier generations. Nonetheless, it's worth noting that Williams, a physician who spent his life dealing with hard fact, could voice his rejection of abstractions only in such abstract terms. Since his time, however, many poets and critics have struggled to reinstall just such language and to define its use in poems. It's understandable, these days, to feel uncertain when competing zealotries struggle not only with each other, but with the perceptions of science and one's own senses. If a young writer should ever ask you, "But what should I do about ideas in my poem," the only serious response is "Yes!"

II

Undercurrents

The Miller's Wife

—Edwin Arlington Robinson

The miller's wife had waited long,
  The tea was cold, the fire was dead;
And there might yet be nothing wrong
  In how he went and what he said:
"There are no millers any more,"
  Was all that she had heard him say;
And he had lingered at the door
  So long that it seemed yesterday.

Sick with a fear that had no form
  She knew that she was there at last;
And in the mill there was a warm
  And mealy fragrance of the past.
What else there was would only seem
  To say again what he had meant;
And what was hanging from a beam
  Would not have heeded where she went.

And if she thought it followed her,
  She may have reasoned in the dark
That one way of the few there were
  Would hide her and would leave no mark:
Black water, smooth above the weir
  Like starry velvet in the night,
Though ruffled once, would soon appear
  The same as ever to the sight.

The Miller's Wife

—de/composed from Robinson

The miller's wife had waited long,
    The tea was cold, the fire was out;
But she hoped there was nothing wrong
    In how he'd left or talked about
How "Mills don't do well anymore."
    That's all that she had heard him say
Though he had lingered at the door
    So long it seemed like yesterday.

Sick with a fear that had no form,
    She knew the truth was waiting there
Inside the mill house where a warm
    And mealy fragrance filled the air;
What else was there she had to hope
    Would tell her fully what he'd meant
And his corpse, hanging from a rope,
    Would never notice where she went.

But if it seemed to follow her,
    She may have thought, there in the dark,
That one of the few ways there were
    To kill herself and leave no mark
Was the black water of the weir—
    Smooth, starry velvet in the night;
'Twould cover her and soon appear
    Calm and unruffled to the sight.

Egyptian Dancer at Shubra

—Bernard Spencer

At first we heard the jingling of her ornaments
as she delayed beyond the trap of light,
and glimpsed her lingering pretence
her bare feet and the music were at difference
and then the strings grew wild and drew her in.

And she came soft as paws and danced desire at play
or triumphing desire, and locked her hands
stretched high, and in the dance's sway
hung like a body to be flogged, then wrenched away,
or was a wave from breasts down to the knees.

And as the music built to climax and she leaned
naked in her dancing skirt, and was supreme,
her dance's stormy argument
had timid workday things for all environment;
men's awkward clothes and chairs her skin exclaimed against.

Belly Dancer

—de/composed from Spencer

At first we heard her necklaces and jewelry
as she waited there outside the spotlight's circle
and still pretended, hesitantly,
that the music and her feet could not keep time
and then the strings grew faster and she entered.

And she came soft as swansdown, dancing like playful lust
or lust triumphant and clenched both her hands
up in the air, then with the music's thrust
poised like an acrobat, twirled as she must,
or undulated from her bust down to her knees.

And as the music grew its wildest, she would sway,
shivering in her dance skirt, and took command
until the thoughts that her dance could expound
attracted the dull everyday objects around—
the human accoutrements her body was opposed to.

A Late Aubade

—Richard Wilbur

You could be sitting now in a carrel
Turning some liver-spotted page,
Or rising in an elevator-cage
Toward Ladies' Apparel.

You could be planting a raucous bed
Of salvia, in rubber gloves,
Or lunching through a screed of someone's loves
With pitying head,

Or making some unhappy setter
Heel, or listening to a bleak
Lecture on Schoenberg's serial technique.
Isn't this better?

Think of the time you are not
Wasting, and would not care to waste,
Such things, thank God, not being to your taste,
Think what a lot

Of time, by woman's reckoning,
You've saved, and so may spend on this,
You who would rather lie in bed and kiss
Than anything.

It's almost noon, you say? If so,
Time flies, and I need not rehearse
The rosebuds-theme of centuries of verse.
If you *must* go,

A Bawdy Noon

—de/composed from Wilbur

You could be hunting through a barrel
Of auto parts for an oil gauge
Or riding escalators, stage by stage,
To buy some Clairol.

You could be in the garden weeding
The lettuce, wearing workmen's gloves,
Or hearing some friend brag on her past loves
And superior breeding

Or teaching some berserk terrier
To fetch, or carrying on a bleak
Affair with someone who's got no technique.
This is lots merrier.

Now's not the time for you to worry
Your little head about the waste
Of time. You know you've got no cause for haste
So what's your hurry?

Just look; the way I see this thing
So much of this day has already gone
We might as well have sex here, on and on
Till evening.

Put down the watch—what *if* it's noon?
So—time flies when you're having fun.
You've heard that flowers fade out with the sun.
Why leave so soon?

A Late Aubade (continued)

Wait for a while, then slip downstairs
And bring us up some chilled white wine,
And some blue cheese, and crackers, and some fine
Ruddy-skinned pears.

A Bawdy Noon (continued)

> You could just trot right downstairs
> And bring me up a little brandy,
> My favorite Swiss cheese and some dandy
> Fat Bartlett pears.

Janet Waking

—John Crowe Ransom

Beautifully Janet slept
Till it was deeply morning. She woke then
And thought about her dainty-feathered hen,
To see how it had kept.

One kiss she gave her mother.
Only a small one gave she to her daddy
Who would have kissed each curl of his shining baby;
No kiss at all for her brother.

"Old Chucky, old Chucky!" she cried,
Running across the world upon the grass
To Chucky's house, and listening. But alas,
Her Chucky had died.

It was a transmogrifying bee
Came droning down on Chucky's old bald head
And sat and put the poison. It scarcely bled,
But how exceedingly

And purply did the knot
Swell with the venom and communicate
Its rigor! Now the poor comb stood up straight
But Chucky did not.

So there was Janet
Kneeling on the wet grass, crying her brown hen
(Translated far beyond the daughters of men)
To rise and walk upon it.

Janet's Pet

—de/composed from Ransom

Janet slept beautifully
Till it was broad daylight. She woke then
And thought about her favorite pet hen
To check how it might be.

One kiss Janet gave her mother
One for her daddy who'd have kissed each curl
Upon the sweet head of his darling girl;
She seldom kissed her brother.

"Old Chucky, old Chucky," she'd say,
Running across the yard, hurrying gladly
To the hen coop and listening, but sadly
Her pet had passed away.

It was only a tiny bee
That flew down onto her pet's unguarded head
And perched to set its sting. It scarcely bled
But how abundantly

The poison flowed to fill
An ugly purple lump and then to spread
And swell out the stiff comb upon its head.
Now Janet's hen lay still.

So there on the muddy ground
Knelt Janet, calling her beloved hen
(Now gone so far beyond the realms of men)
To get up and walk around.

Janet Waking (continued)

And weeping fast as she had breath
Janet implored us, "Wake her from her sleep!"
And would not be instructed in how deep
Was the forgetful kingdom of death.

Janet's Pet (continued)

And weeping, with her choked breath
Janet implored us, "But she's slept too long!"
And would not hear us telling her how strong
Was the merciless kingdom of death.

Piazza Piece

—John Crowe Ransom

—I am a gentleman in a dust coat trying
To make you hear. Your ears are soft and small
And listen to an old man not at all,
They want the young men's whispering and sighing.
But see the roses on your trellis dying
And hear the spectral singing of the moon;
For I must have my lovely lady soon,
I am a gentleman in a dust coat trying.

—I am a lady young in beauty waiting
Until my truelove comes, and then we kiss.
But what gray man among the vines is this
Whose words are dry and faint as in a dream?
Back from my trellis, Sir, before I scream!
I am a lady young in beauty waiting.

Death and the Maiden

—de/composed from Ransom

—My name is Death and I've come in disguise
To talk to you. Your ears are flat and small
And will not hear the things I say at all;
They want somebody's whisperings and sighs.
But think of how the lovely rose soon dies
And understand the message of the moon
For I will have to take you with me soon;
My name is Death and I've come in disguise.

—I am a fair young Maiden, waiting here
For my true lover so we can embrace;
But who has come, intruding his gray face
And voice, like words in dreams, gone faint and dry?
Just leave my garden, Sir, or else I'll cry!
I am a fair young Maiden, waiting here.

Sonnet #73

—William Shakespeare

That time of year thou mayst in me behold
When yellow leaves, or none, or few, do hang
Upon those boughs which shake against the cold,
Bare ruined choirs,[1] where late the sweet birds sang.
In me thou see'st the twilight of such day
As after sunset fadeth in the west,
Which by and by black night doth take away,
Death's second self, that seals up all in rest.
In me thou see'st the glowing of such fire
That on the ashes of his youth doth lie,
As the death-bed whereon it must expire,
Consumed with that which it was nourished by.
    This thou perceivest, which makes thy love more strong,
    To love that well which thou must leave ere long.

↻ Sonnet #73

—de/composed from Shakespeare

That time of year thou mayst in me behold
When foliage takes flight and leaves the tree
So leafless boughs are subject to the cold
Where summer birds made music formerly.
In me thou mayst behold how light can fade
That once shone brightly all across the sky
But as time passes turns to deepening shade

---

[1] Choir lofts.

Declining to Death's darkness by and by.
In me you see how fires burned down may be
Still bright above the fuel already burned
Although the fire must go out finally,
Consumed by getting that for which it yearned.
    This thou perceivest though not turned cold thereby
    And love me more though soon I have to die.

Sonnet #73

—re/de/composed from Shakespeare

I've reached an age when everybody sees
Signs that I'm old, no young growth anymore
Or vigor in my frail extremities—
Ruins that were so full of life before.
In me is seen fading vitality
As if now aging powers have declined
Till they will soon have vanished totally
In death which no slightest thing behind.
Such remnants of past strengths appear in me
As have used up their former youthful forces
And now they wait to give up utterly
Having exhausted all of their resources.
    And yet your love for me grows even stronger
    Knowing I've got to go before much longer.

Sailing to Byzantium

—William Butler Yeats

I

That is no country for old men. The young
In one another's arms, birds in the trees,
—Those dying generations—at their song,
The salmon-falls, the mackerel-crowded seas,
Fish, flesh, or fowl, commend all summer long
Whatever is begotten, born, and dies.
Caught in that sensual music all neglect
Monuments of unageing intellect.

II

An aged man is but a paltry thing,
A tattered coat upon a stick, unless
Soul clap its hands and sing, and louder sing
For every tatter in its mortal dress,
Nor is there singing school but studying
Monuments of its own magnificence;
And therefore I have sailed the seas and come
To the holy city of Byzantium.

III

O sages standing in God's holy fire
As in the gold mosaic of a wall,
Come from the holy fire, perne[1] in a gyre,
And be the singing-masters of my soul.
Consume my heart away; sick with desire
And fastened to a dying animal

---

[1]Cultist term for "turn" or "spiral."

Elderhostel in the East

—de/composed from Yeats

I

Old Ireland's not a place the old should go.
The young make love, birds mate in all the trees—
Live generations sing the songs they know
Of salmon streams and mackerel-crowded seas
While birds and beasts commend their whole lives long
Whatever's full of passion till it dies.
Entrapped in sensuous music all neglect
The old with their maturing intellect.

II

An aged man is but a loveless thing,
A tattered bag of skin and bones, unless
The soul puts off its robes of flesh to sing
With pure, eternal radiance for its dress,
Nor is there cause for song but studying
The soul in its austere magnificence;
So I have left the Western world and come
To see the city of Byzantium.

III

You sages standing in a holy fire
Shown in the gold mosaic of a wall
That by your chaste example can inspire
And teach eternal wisdom to my soul,
Come, quench my heart of yearning and desire
For, trapped inside a dying animal,

Sailing to Byzantium (continued)

It knows not what it is; and gather me
Into the artifice of eternity.

IV

Once out of nature I shall never take
My bodily form from any natural thing,
But such a form as Grecian goldsmiths make
Of hammered gold and gold enameling
To keep a drowsy Emperor awake;
Or set upon a golden bough to sing
To lords and ladies of Byzantium
Of what is past, or passing, or to come.

It only wants the saints to gather me
Into a fixed, eternal unity.

IV

Once freed from passion I shall never take
My heart's design from any aging thing,
But such as Grecian goldsmiths strove to make
Of precious gold and gold enameling
To soothe a lovesick Emperor's heartache;
Or mount upon a golden stage to sing
To all the people that Byzantium
Is where the sick and elderly should come.

A Supermarket in California

—Allen Ginsberg

What thoughts I have of you tonight, Walt Whitman, for I walked down the sidestreets under the trees with a headache self-conscious looking at the full moon.

In my hungry fatigue, and shopping for images, I went into the neon fruit supermarket, dreaming of your enumerations!

What peaches and what penumbras! Whole families shopping at night! Aisles full of husbands! Wives in the avocados, babies in the tomatoes!—and you, García Lorca, what were you doing down by the watermelons?

I saw you, Walt Whitman, childless, lonely old grubber, poking among the meats in the refrigerator and eyeing the grocery boys.

I heard you asking questions of each: Who killed the pork chops? What price bananas? Are you my Angel?

I wandered in and out of the brilliant stacks of cans following you, and followed in my imagination by the store detective.

We strode down the open corridors together in our solitary fancy tasting artichokes, possessing every frozen delicacy, and never passing the cashier.

Where are we going, Walt Whitman? The doors close in an hour. Which way does your beard point tonight?

(I touch your book and dream of our odyssey in the supermarket and feel absurd.)

Will we walk all night through solitary streets? The trees add shade to shade, lights out in the houses, we'll both be lonely.

Will we stroll dreaming of the lost America of love past blue automobiles in driveways, home to our silent cottage?

A Produce Market in California

—de/composed from Ginsberg

What thoughts I have of you tonight, Walt Whitman, for I walked
down the streets cheerful self-confident, looking at the full moon.

In my good mood, and shopping for images, I went into the neon
produce market, dreaming of your lists!
What oranges and aureoles! Whole office staffs shopping at night!
Aisles full of lawyers! agents in the mangoes! typists in the pears!—and
you, Bertolt Brecht, what were you doing down by the watermelons?

I saw you, Walt Whitman, jobless, friendly old geezer, poking among
the packages in the refrigerator and bothering the clerks.
I heard you asking questions of each: Who killed the pork chops?
What price broccoli? Have you found salvation?
I wandered in and out of the brilliant stacks of cans following you,
and followed in my imagination by the janitor.
We strode down the close rows together in a communal spirit tasting
grapes, trying every aged cheese, and never passing the exit.

Where are we going, Walt Whitman? The doors close in an hour. Does
your beard point toward home tonight?
(I touch your book and dream of our odyssey in the produce market
and feel exuberant.)
Will we walk all night through festive streets? The trees add leaf to
leaf, lights gleam in the houses, we'll both feel contented.
Will we stroll relishing the new America of affluence past red
automobiles in parking lots, home to our cozy cottage?

A Supermarket in California (continued)

Ah, dear father, graybeard, lonely old courage-teacher, what America did you have when Charon quit poling his ferry and you got out on a smoking bank and stood watching the boat disappear on the black waters of Lethe?

Ah, dear father, graybeard, lively old joy-teacher, what America did you need when Charon quit poling his ferry and you got out on a green bank and stood seeing the boat bob on the calm waters of the River Styx?

Nantucket

—William Carlos Williams

Flowers through the window
lavender and yellow

changed by white curtains—
Smell of cleanliness—

Sunshine of late afternoon—
On the glass tray

a glass pitcher, the tumbler
turned down, by which

a key is lying—And the
immaculate white bed

Nantucket

—de/composed from Williams

Flowers through the open window
purple and golden

glowing beyond the heavy drapes—
scent of detergents—

sunshine of high noon—
on the silvery tray

a silver teapot, the cup
upturned by which

a spoon is placed—and the
fresh linen tablecloth.

Transformations

—Thomas Hardy

Portion of this yew
Is a man my grandsire knew,
Bosomed here at its foot:
This branch may be his wife,
A ruddy human life
Now turned to a green shoot.

These grasses must be made
Of her who often prayed,
Last century, for repose;
And the fair girl long ago
Whom I vainly tried to know
May be entering this rose.

So, they are not underground,
But as nerves and veins abound
In the growths of upper air,
And they feel the sun and rain,
And the energy again
That made them what they were!

Resurrections

—de/composed from Hardy

Some part of this yew
Is a man my grandad knew
Mounded here at its foot:
This branch may be his wife,
A humble human life
Now turned to a leaf or fruit.

These grasses must be she
Who prayed, last century,
For peace after life's woes;
And the girl, fair and sweet,
I had often tried to meet
Is reborn in this rose.

So now they are not gone
But as nerves and veins live on
As creatures of this earth,
Experience sun and rain,
And the Providence again
That grants them this rebirth!

Afterwards

—Thomas Hardy

When the Present has latched its postern behind my tremulous stay,
    And the May month flaps its glad green leaves like wings,
Delicate-filmed as new-spun silk, will the neighbours say,
    "He was a man who used to notice such things"?

If it be in the dusk when, like an eyelid's soundless blink,
    The dewfall-hawk comes crossing the shades to alight
Upon the wind-warped upland thorn, a gazer may think,
    "To him this must have been a familiar sight."

If I pass during some nocturnal blackness, mothy and warm,
    When the hedgehog travels furtively over the lawn,
One may say, "He strove that such innocent creatures should come to no harm,
    But he could do little for them; and now he is gone."

If, when hearing that I have been stilled at last, they stand at the door,
    Watching the full-starred heavens that winter sees,
Will this thought rise on those who will meet my face no more,
    "He was one who had an eye for such mysteries"?

And will any say when my bell of quittance is heard in the gloom,
    And a crossing breeze cuts a pause in its outrollings,
Till they rise again, as they were a new bell's boom,
    "He hears it not now, but used to notice such things"?

The End

—de/composed from Hardy

When the Present has latched its postern behind my hesitant stay,
    And November flaps its dry, stiff leaves like wings
Of leathery-tough black bats, will the neighbours say,
    "He was a man who used to notice such things?"

If it be at day's end when, as an eye might silently close,
    The nightfall hawk comes out of deepening shades to dive
Onto the wind-warped upland oak, some may suppose,
    "He must have often seen such sights when alive."

If I die during some night's utter blackness, sterile and chill,
    When the house cat slips out, prowling for prey in the wood,
One may say, "He strove that we might live one with Nature still,
    Yet great forests get cleared; now he, too, is gone for good."

If, sometime after I have died, they stand at their door,
    Watching the sky's blank space that winter sees
Will it occur to those who will meet my face no more,
    "He was one who had an eye for sights like these"?

And will any say when my death bell tolls in the gloom
    Till its sound is silenced by a quick shift of the breeze,
But then they hear some different bell's more distant boom,
    "He nevermore will listen to such sounds as these"?

The Man He Killed

—Thomas Hardy

"Had he and I but met
        By some old ancient inn,
We should have sat us down to wet
        Right many a nipperkin![1]

"But ranged as infantry,
        And staring face to face,
I shot at him as he at me,
        And killed him in his place.

"I shot him dead because—
        Because he was my foe,
Just so: my foe of course he was;
        That's clear enough; although

"He thought he'd 'list, perhaps,
        Off-hand like—just as I—
Was out of work—had sold his traps—
        No other reason why.

"Yes; quaint and curious war is!
        You shoot a fellow down
You'd treat if met where any bar is,
        Or help to half-a-crown."

------

[1]Have many small drinks.

The Stanza He Killed

—de/composed from Hardy

"Had he and I but met
By some familiar inn,
We might have sat us down to wet
Our tongues with rum or gin!

"But ranged as infantry,
I stared straight in his eye
And shot before he shot at me,
And there I let him lie.

"I shot him dead because
He was my country's foe;
That's just exactly what he was
And yet for all I know

"He thought he'd 'list, perhaps—
A lot of others did that, too—
Was out of work—had sold his traps—
That's all he meant to do.

"How vile and terrible is war!
You feel no qualms at killing
Men you'd buy drinks at any bar
Or lend them crowns and shillings."

Traveling through the Dark

—William Stafford

Traveling through the dark I found a deer
dead on the edge of the Wilson River road.
It is usually best to roll them into the canyon:
that road is narrow; to swerve might make more dead.

By glow of the tail-light I stumbled back of the car
and stood by the heap, a doe, a recent killing;
she had stiffened already, almost cold.
I dragged her off; she was large in the belly.

My fingers touching her side brought me the reason—
her side was warm; her fawn lay there waiting,
alive, still, never to be born.
Beside that mountain road I hesitated.

The car aimed ahead its lowered parking lights;
under the hood purred the steady engine.
I stood in the glare of the warm exhaust turning red;
around our group I could hear the wilderness listen.

I thought hard for us all—my only swerving—,
then pushed her over the edge into the river.

Driving Late at Night

—de/composed from Stafford

Driving late at night I found an animal
that had been killed on the road.
I always drag such things off the pavement—
that road's hazardous; if a car swerves it's a danger.

In the darkness I walked back of the car
to examine the body, a female, not dead for long
though rigor mortis was setting in, the body warmth going.
When I moved her, she was surprisingly heavy.

I soon found out why—
she was pregnant; the unborn foetus
was still alive but irrecoverable.
On that steep road I took just long enough to decide.

I knew I needed to go ahead
with the errands I'd started out on.
There was a lot of pressure since
I wanted to be sure I did the right thing.

I weighed all factors but wasn't indecisive
and shoved the corpse over the cliff for good and all.

Piano

—D. H. Lawrence
(final version, 1918)

Softly, in the dusk, a woman is singing to me;
Taking me back down the vista of years, till I see
A child sitting under the piano, in the boom of the tingling strings
And pressing the small, poised feet of a mother who smiles as she sings.

In spite of myself, the insidious mastery of song
Betrays me back, till the heart of me weeps to belong
To the old Sunday evenings at home, with winter outside
And hymns in the cozy parlor, the tinkling piano our guide.

So now it is vain for the singer to burst into clamour
With the great black piano appassionato.[1] The glamour
Of childish days is upon me, my manhood is cast
Down in the flood of remembrance, I weep like a child for the past.

---

[1]Musical direction: "passionately."

↻ Pianola

—de/composed from Lawrence

All day, through the house, a woman is singing to me;
Taking me back down the vista of years till I see
A child sitting under the piano, in the boom of resounding strings
Close to the bright black shoes of a mother who smiles as she sings.

I wonder, amazed, as the marvelous mastery of song
Carries me back, till the heart of me weeps to belong
To the old Sunday evenings at home, while rain falls outside,
With songs in the well-lit parlor, the cheerful piano our guide.

So now I am thrilled when the singer bursts forth strong and pure
With the great loud piano fortissimo. The allure
Of childhood days returns to me, the present is cast
Off in the flood of remembrance; I weep to return to the past.

The Piano

—Lawrence's first version, from notebook, 1907–8(?)
(canceled words symbolized by <> and italicized)

Somewhere beneath that piano's superb sleek black
Must hide my mother's piano, little and brown, with the back stood close to
That <*was against*> the wall, and the front's faded silk, both torn,
And the keys with little hollows, that my mother's fingers had worn.

Softly, in the shadows, a woman is singing to me
Quietly, through the years I have crept back to see
A child sitting under the piano, in the boom of the shaking <*tingling*> strings
Pressing the little poised feet of the mother who smiles as she sings

The full throated woman has chosen a winning, tiny [?] song
And surely the heart that is in me must belong
To the old Sunday evenings, when darkness wandered outside
And hymns gleamed on our warm lips, as we watched mother's fingers glide

          is
Or <*is*> this / my sister at home in the old front room
Singing love's first surprised gladness, alone in the gloom.
She will start when she sees me, and blushing, spread out her hands
To cover my mouth's raillery, till I'm bound in her heart-spun shame's
    <*pleading*> bands.

A woman is singing me a wild Hungarian air
And her arms, and her bosom, and the whole of her soul is bare
And the great black piano is clamouring as my mother's never could clamour
        my mother's <*songs tunes*> tunes are
And the <*the tune/s of the past is*> devoured of this music's ravaging glamour.

II. Undercurrents

"The secret of being perfectly dull," said my professor, winking broadly, "is to answer all the questions." If art imitates life, some problems must remain unsolved, some questions unanswered; even the simplest declaration may require alert and sensitive interpretation. In ordinary conversation, as much as 85 percent of our meaning lies not in the literal sense of words, but in our tone of voice, inflection, expression, stance, or body carriage. Friends say, "Yeah, right!" and we understand, "No way!" E. E. Cummings writes, "Humanity i love you" while Sir Thomas Wyatt writes, "Sins that I so kindely am served" and we know that they, too, mean just the opposite.

Poetry deals particularly with the implicit, with what is open to question, and must do so without body language or designated vocal qualities. The printed text must enrich and complicate its "message content" through such factors as implied tones of voice, levels of language and usage, connotations, ambiguities, suggestions, contexts, literary and cultural references, musicality, and sound textures. Like the subtext of a play, these matters are open to interpretation and opinion. This becomes obvious if we look at poetry translations: literal or dictionary renderings often seem no poem at all. Knowing only a literal translation of a poem written in English, a foreign reader might well get nothing better than what these de/compositions offer.

In Robinson's "The Miller's Wife," we find a vital clash between the propriety of language and the dreadful events related. This is, after all, an aspect of dramatic characterization; most of us tend to shield frightening facts in euphemisms. For the reader, this offers the added excitement of suspicion and discovery. Bernard Spencer's "Egyptian Dancer at Shubra" similarly balances a proper tone against hints of a bestial sensuality in the dancer and of a sadistic lust in her audience.

Much of our enjoyment in Richard Wilbur's "A Late Aubade" lies in characterization by suggestion—implying what needn't be bluntly mouthed. The speaker, coaxing his partner to stay in bed, courts her with imaginative wit and sophistry; my version's speaker might as well boot her out onto the floor. Just as Wilbur shows a due respect for the lady's—and our—ability to read a coded language, John Crowe Ransom's poems assume we can appreciate the affectionate ironies of "Janet Waking" and the gentle mockery with which "Piazza Piece" parodies the old fable of Death and the Maiden.

William Shakespeare's "Sonnet #73" opens with one of the most brilliant quatrains in the language. Embodying the speaker's age in the trees' seasonal change, the poem then transforms those branches into the choir lofts of ruined churches. This tells us little about the facts of aging but much about the speaker's emotions. Although the poem laments the speaker's fading powers of song, it does so in superbly lively language; to demonstrate enfeebled abilities would surely delight no one.

Many poems in this collection deal with events which are presented as autobiographical: Elizabeth Spires's "Globe" (p. 8), William Stafford's "Traveling through the Dark" (p. 70), Wallace Stevens's "Anecdote of the Jar" (p. 102), or Theodore Roethke's "My Papa's Waltz" (p. 144). Our interest as readers, however, lies not in an accurate rendering of facts and events but in broader matters that reveal the speaker's sense of the world. Certainly, some knowledge of the poet's life, beliefs, literary influences, other writings may prove useful to a reader. For instance, one reads much of W. B. Yeats's later work—including "Sailing to Byzantium" and "The Second Coming"—more effectively if aware of his system of occult belief in the cyclical nature of human history.

Even so, such knowledge can sometimes prove not only distracting, but downright misleading—many splendid poems reveal the writer's emotions rising up to oppose his or her conscious beliefs. Many of Allen Ginsberg's poems and public statements proudly flaunt his homosexuality. Yet "A Supermarket in California," one of his best-known poems, betrays strong feelings of anguish and guilt. D. H. Lawrence is widely known as advocating a wider, more active sexuality, yet "Piano" (p. 72) records an impotence brought on by recollection of the speaker's ties to his mother. Similarly, William Carlos Williams wrote many poems in praise of sexual vigor, a random fertility and/or promiscuity, yet "Nantucket" surprises us—and may have surprised him—by its appreciation of purity and an apparent chastity.

In his own time, Thomas Hardy's agnosticism created considerable scandal. Yet such poems as "Afterwards" and "Transformations" (or "The Oxen," quoted in Section III) show not only that he very much *wanted* to believe but that much of his religious background still remained with him. "The Man He Killed" obviously means us to find war not merely "quaint and curious." Nonetheless, it is more effective to reach that conclusion through the thoughts of an ordinary ex-soldier who hesitantly approaches a higher morality while struggling also to preserve his patriotic beliefs.

William Stafford's "Traveling through the Dark" portrays a world of strong moral imperatives, yet of great uncertainty. On one side, we feel a need for a responsible concern for others' safety; on the other, that may impose painful choices. Meantime, we are given no reliable directions or assurance of final good and evil. The de/composition's speaker, in contrast, is full of self-righteous, self-admiring certainty.

III

The Singular Voice

A Narrow Fellow in the Grass

—Emily Dickinson

A narrow Fellow in the Grass
Occasionally rides—
You may have met Him—did you not
His notice[1] sudden is—

The Grass divides as with a Comb—
A spotted shaft is seen—
And then it closes at your feet
And opens further on—

He likes a Boggy Acre
A Floor too cool for Corn—
Yet when a Boy, and Barefoot—
I more than once at Noon
Have passed, I thought, a Whip lash
Unbraiding in the Sun
When stooping to secure it
It wrinkled, and was gone—

Several of Nature's People
I know, and they know me—
I feel for them a transport
Of cordiality—

But never met this Fellow
Attended, or alone
Without a tighter breathing
And Zero at the Bone—

---

[1] Either your notice of him or his giving notice of departure (as of a renter).

A Slender Creature

—de/composed from Dickinson

A slender creature through the grass
Occasionally slides;
You may have seen him but if not,
Away he swiftly glides.

The grass divides itself in two;
You see a spotted form
And then it closes near to you
And opens further on.

He likes a marshy meadow,
A floor too cool for corn,
Yet when a child out walking
I more than once at noon
Have passed what seemed a whip lash
Discarded in the sun
But when I stooped to get it
It wriggled and was gone.

Many of nature's creatures
Are quite well known to me;
I feel for them a sense of
Familiarity

Yet never met this creature
Alone or with friends near
But, frightened, caught my breath
And felt the grip of fear.

If I Shouldn't Be Alive

—Emily Dickinson

If I shouldn't be alive
When the Robins come,
Give the one in Red Cravat,
A Memorial crumb.

If I couldn't thank you,
Being fast asleep,
You will know I'm trying
With my Granite lip!

If I Should Not Survive

          —de/composed from Dickinson, A

If I should not survive
Until the robins come,
Give the one whose breast's bright red
A memorial crumb.

If I couldn't thank you
Since I passed away,
You will know I'm trying
With my lips of clay.

When The Robins Come

          —de/composed from Dickinson, B

When the robins come
If I should be dead
In my remembrance give a crumb
To the one whose breast is red.

If I couldn't thank you,
Since I am cold and dead,
You will know I'm trying
With my tongue of lead.

I Heard a Fly Buzz—When I Died

—Emily Dickinson

I heard a Fly buzz—when I died—
The Stillness in the Room
Was like the Stillness in the Air—
Between the Heaves of Storm—

The Eyes around—had wrung them dry—
And Breaths were gathering firm
For that last Onset—when the King
Be witnessed—in the Room—

I willed my Keepsakes—Signed away
What portion of me be
Assignable—and then it was
There interposed a Fly—

With Blue—uncertain stumbling Buzz—
Between the light—and me—
And then the Windows failed—and then
I could not see to see—

A Fly Got in the Day I Died

—de/composed from Dickinson

A fly got in, the day I died;
The calm in my bedroom
Was like the quiet in the air
Between the blasts of storm.

The eyes around had all gone dry;
Everyone held their breath
To see the presence in the room
Of Life's great ruler, Death.

I gave my worldly goods away,
Willed every part of me
That could be willed—and then it was
That suddenly appeared the fly,

Uncertain, stumbling, blue; its buzz
Dimmed out the light from me
And then the windows failed, and then
I could no longer see.

The Oxen

—Thomas Hardy

Christmas Eve, and twelve of the clock,
    "Now they are all on their knees,"
An elder said as we sat in a flock
    By the embers in hearthside ease.

We pictured the meek mild creatures where
    They dwelt in their strawy pen,
Nor did it occur to one of us there
    To doubt they were kneeling then.

So fair a fancy few would weave
    In these years! Yet, I feel,
If someone said on Christmas Eve,
    "Come; see the oxen kneel,

"In the lonely barton[1] by yonder coomb[2]
    Our childhood used to know,"
I should go with him in the gloom,
    Hoping it might be so.

---

[1] British rural dialect: farmstead.
[2] British rural dialect: hollow or valley.

↻ # Oxen

—de/composed from Hardy

Christmas Eve, and twelve of the clock,
    "The oxen are all on their knees,"
A teacher said as we sat to talk
    By the embers in hearthside ease.

We thought of those great, strong creatures where
    They lived in their strawy pen,
Nor did it occur to one of us there
    That they might not be kneeling then.

In times like these, no one would weave
    Such stories! Yet I know
If someone said on Christmas Eve,
    "Come now and let's all go

See the oxen kneel in the stable's straw
    As we heard they did long ago,"
I should go with him, filled with awe,
    Convinced that it was so.

Drummer Hodge

—Thomas Hardy

I

They throw in Drummer Hodge, to rest
    Uncoffined—just as found:
His landmark is a kopje-crest[1]
    That breaks the veldt[2] around;
And foreign constellations west
    Each night above his mound.

II

Young Hodge the Drummer never knew—
    Fresh from his Wessex home—
The meaning of the broad Karoo,[3]
    The Bush, the dusty loam,
And why uprose to nightly view
    Strange stars amid the gloom.

III

Yet portion of that unknown plain
    Will Hodge for ever be;
His homely Northern breast and brain
    Grow to some Southern tree,
And strange-eyed constellations reign
    His stars eternally.

---

[1] South African dialect: hilltop.
[2] South African dialect: open grazing land.
[3] South African dialect: arid plateau.

Drummer Vaughan

—de/composed from Hardy

I

They throw in Drummer Vaughan to rest
    Uncoffined, just as found;
His landmark is a little crest
    That marks the landscape 'round,
And strange stars circle toward the west
    Each night above his mound.

II

Young Vaughan the Drummer never knew—
    Fresh from his London home—
The meaning of that country's hue,
    The woods he had to roam,
Or why strange stars rose into view
    Each night in heaven's dome.

III

A part, though, of that foreign plain
    Vaughan will now come to be;
His simple English heart and brain
    Become some tropic tree;
Strange constellations will remain
    Above him endlessly.

God's Grandeur

—Gerard Manley Hopkins

The world is charged with the grandeur of God.
    It will flame out, like shining from shook foil;
    It gathers to a greatness, like the ooze of oil
Crushed. Why do men then now not reck his rod?
Generations have trod, have trod, have trod;
    And all is seared with trade; bleared, smeared with toil;
    And wears man's smudge and shares man's smell: the soil
Is bare now, nor can foot feel, being shod.

And for all this, nature is never spent;
    There lives the dearest freshness deep down things;
And though the last lights off the black West went
    Oh, morning, at the brown brink eastward, springs—
Because the Holy Ghost over the bent
    World broods with warm breast and with ah! bright wings.

God's Grandeur

—de/composed from Hopkins

The world's full of the glory of the Lord.
    It will appear like sparks from shaken foil;
    It grows to have great force like compressed oil.
Yet why, among men, is His word ignored?
Man's generations on and on have trod;
    Our greed and toil rob everything of worth;
    Things come to have man's mark and smell. The earth
Is bare, yet men feel nothing since they're shod.

And yet the world is filled with rich supplies;
    There is a lovely freshness inside things;
What though, in darkness Westward, twilight dies,
    At the horizon Eastward morning springs—
The Holy Ghost o'er the prone world will rise
    With His warm breast and His bright-colored wings.

Sonnet #67

—Gerard Manley Hopkins

I wake and feel the fell of dark, not day.
What hours, O what black hoürs we have spent
This night! what sights you, heart, saw; ways you went!
And more must, in yet longer light's delay.

With witness I speak this. But where I say
Hours I mean years, mean life. And my lament
Is cries countless, cries like dead letters sent
To dearest him that lives alas! away.

I am gall, I am heartburn. God's most deep decree
Bitter would have me taste: my taste was me;
Bones built in me, flesh filled, blood brimmed the curse.

Selfyeast of spirit a dull dough sours. I see
The lost are like this, and their scourge to be
As I am mine, their sweating selves; but worse.

Sonnet #67

—de/composed from Hopkins

I wake and feel that night has come, not day.
This night, what long dark hours we have spent!
What sights you saw, my heart, what ways you went!
And must endure more during light's delay.

I have strong witness for this. When I say
Hours it's really years, life. And my lament
Is like unending cries, or letters sent
To one's dear love who lives far, far away.

I'm filled with bitterness. The Lord's decree
Instilled a bitter taste through all of me.
My whole existence has fulfilled the curse.

This life's bread swells up sour. The lost, I see
Are like this and it is their scourge to be
Their selves as I am mine, but even worse.

A Refusal to Mourn the Death, by Fire, of a Child in London

—Dylan Thomas

Never until the mankind making
Bird beast and flower
Fathering and all humbling darkness
Tells with silence the last light breaking
And the still hour
Is come of the sea tumbling in harness

And I must enter again the round
Zion of the water bead
And the synagogue of the ear of corn
Shall I let pray the shadow of a sound
Or sow my salt seed
In the least valley of sackcloth to mourn

The majesty and burning of the child's death.
I shall not murder
The mankind of her going with a grave truth
Nor blaspheme down the stations of the breath
With any further
Elegy of innocence and youth.

Deep with the first dead lies London's daughter,
Robed in the long friends,
The grains beyond age, the dark veins of her mother,
Secret by the unmourning water
Of the riding[1] Thames.
After the first death, there is no other.

-----
[1] Archaic term for the sex act.

Grieving for the Death,
by Fire, of a Child in London

—de/composed from Thomas

Never until the darkness that creates
Bird, beast and flower,
As well as mankind and so humbles everything
Announces silently the last burst of light
And the sea wallowing in its boundaries
Has reached its time to stand still

And I must enter again the holy
Homeland of the water bead
And the worship of the vegetation,
Shall I let myself pray even one word's echo
Or let fall one tear
In the smallest gulf of mourning

For the horror and suffering of her dying.
I shall not desecrate
The universality of her death with falsehoods
Nor defile the body's processes
With any
Lament for her pure qualities.

The London girl lies with prehistoric bodies,
Furnished with age-old allies,
The timeless nourishments, the heritage of humankind,
Hidden near the carefree water
Of the fertilizing Thames.
Having died once, you live forever.

The Force That Through the Green Fuse Drives the Flower

—Dylan Thomas

The force that through the green fuse drives the flower
Drives my green age; that blasts the roots of trees
Is my destroyer.
And I am dumb to tell the crooked rose
My youth is bent by the same wintry fever.

The force that drives the water through the rocks
Drives my red blood; that dries the mouthing streams
Turns mine to wax.
And I am dumb to mouth unto my veins
How at the mountain spring the same mouth sucks.

The hand that whirls the water in the pool
Stirs the quicksand; that ropes the blowing wind
Hauls my shroud sail.
And I am dumb to tell the hanging man
How of my clay is made the hangman's lime.

The lips of time leech to the fountain head;
Love drips and gathers, but the fallen blood
Shall calm her sores.
And I am dumb to tell a weather's wind
How time has ticked a heaven round the stars.

And I am dumb to tell the lover's tomb
How at my sheet goes the same crooked worm.

The Tendency That Draws Flowers from Their Stalk

—de/composed from Thomas

The tendency that draws flowers from their stalk
Impels my growth; whatever ruins trees' roots
Destroys me too.
And it does not content the damaged rose
That the same sterile turmoil twists my youth.

The same pressure that pushes water through rocks
Pumps my bloodstream; what dries up babbling brooks
Coagulates my blood.
And my blood vessels find no comfort
That what draws my circulation draws mountain springs.

Water's proclivity to rotate, running out,
Helps form quicksand; whatever controls winds
Propels me from and toward death.
And I cannot explain to the corpse
That my life, too, decomposes my flesh.

Year after year, life's source is drained away;
Love comes and goes but approaching death
Will soothe its pain.
And I cannot convince the changing seasons
That passing seconds build eternity beyond our galaxy.

And I cannot console the long-dead lover
That the same warped appetites break down my body.

Repose of Rivers

—Hart Crane

The willows carried a slow sound,
A sarabande the wind mowed on the mead.
I could never remember
That seething, steady leveling of the marshes
Till age had brought me to the sea.

Flags, weeds. And remembrance of steep alcoves
Where cypresses shared the noon's
Tyranny; they drew me into hades almost.
And mammoth turtles climbing sulphur dreams
Yielded, while sun-silt rippled them
Asunder . . .

How much I would have bartered! the black gorge
And all the singular nestings in the hills
Where beavers learn stitch and tooth.
The pond I entered once and quickly fled—
I remember now its singing willow rim.

And finally, in that memory all things nurse;
After the city that I finally passed
With scalding unguents spread and smoking darts
The monsoon cut across the delta
At gulf gates . . . There, beyond the dykes

I heard wind flaking sapphire, like this summer,
And willows could not hold more steady sound.

↻ Placid Waters

—de/composed from Crane

There was a dull murmur in the trees,
A solemn dance the air currents made through the fields.
I've always kept forgetting how
Everything is washed and evenly worn down in swamplands
Till getting older brought me back to the shore.

Reeds; underbrush. And memories of high nooks
Where slender trees were also battered by
Midday sun; they dragged me nearly to doom.
And thick-shelled sea beasts climbing acrid visions
Gave up, while heat corroded them
Into particles.

How much I would have traded! that deep gully
And all the distinctive lodgings in the hills
Where young animals learn to build and tear things down.
The pool I stepped into once then ran away—
I still think of its border of murmuring trees.

In the end, to remember that cures everything.
After leaving the urban scene and a society
Full of harmful medicines and inflaming gibes,
The weather pattern moved across the tidal flats
That open out to sea. There, beyond the breakwaters

I heard the wind scattering blue crystals, like this summer,
And trees could not contain a calmer tone.

At Melville's Tomb

—Hart Crane

Often beneath the wave, wide from this ledge
The dice of drowned men's bones he saw bequeath
An embassy. Their numbers as he watched,
Beat on the dusty shore and were obscured.

And wrecks passed without sound of bells,
The calyx of death's bounty giving back
A scattered chapter, livid hieroglyph,
The portent wound in corridors of shells.

Then in the circuit calm of one vast coil,
Its lashings charmed and malice reconciled,
Frosted eyes there were that lifted altars;
And silent answers crept across the stars.

Compass, quadrant and sextant contrive
No further tides . . . High in the azure steeps
Monody shall not wake the mariner.
This fabulous shadow only the sea keeps.

At Melville's Tomb

—de/composed from Crane

He often saw—underseas, far offshore—
The random fortune of men's catastrophes
Giving him a purpose. As he watched, their diverse fates
With all accounts of them were lost

While disasters happened without rites of mourning,
The source of so many deaths yielding
Fragments of meaning, dangerous signs,
The warning seen in other species' remains.

Then in the peace returning after great tribulation—
Its torments soothed and evils justified—
The vision of some of the long dead created a religion
And explanations for the universe appeared.

Celestial navigation devices will not prepare us
For future circumstances. High in the heavens
This traveler will not respond to my song.
This great soul is found only in the sea.

Anecdote of the Jar

—Wallace Stevens

I placed a jar in Tennessee,
And round it was, upon a hill.
It made the slovenly wilderness
Surround that hill.

The wilderness rose up to it,
And sprawled around, no longer wild.
The jar was round upon the ground
And tall and of a port in air.

It took dominion everywhere.
The jar was gray and bare.
It did not give of[1] bird or bush,
Like nothing else in Tennessee.

---

[1]Give suggestions of.

Anecdote of the Jar

—de/composed from Stevens

I dropped a jar on a hill
In Tennessee—a round jar.
Because of it, the overgrown backwoods
Took positions relative to that hill.

The boondocks grew up toward it
And lay there, tamed.
It was a round jar, flat on the ground,
Large, having a presence in space.

It established standards on all sides.
In itself, it was dull and plain.
It didn't suggest birds or bushes
As everything else in Tennessee did.

Thirteen Ways of Looking at a Blackbird

—Wallace Stevens

I

Among twenty snowy mountains,
The only moving thing
Was the eye of the blackbird.

II

I was of three minds,
Like a tree
In which there are three blackbirds.

III

The blackbird whirled in the autumn winds.
It was a small part of the pantomime.

IV

A man and a woman
Are one.
A man and a woman and a blackbird
Are one.

V

I do not know which to prefer,
The beauty of inflections
Or the beauty of innuendoes,
The blackbird whistling
Or just after.

Various Ways of Looking at Blackbirds

—de/composed from Stevens

I

Among mountains in winter,
The blackbird's eye
Moved though nothing else did.

II

Like a tree
With three blackbirds in it,
I had three choices.

III

Like part of a pantomime,
In the autumn winds the blackbird whirled.

IV

A man and a woman
Can be part of each other.
A man and a women and a blackbird
Can be part of each other.

V

I do not know which is better,
Beautiful phrases—
The blackbird whistling—
Or else suggestions:
The pause afterwards.

VI

Icicles filled the long window
With barbaric glass.
The shadow of the blackbird
Crossed it, to and fro.
The mood
Traced in the shadow
An indecipherable cause.

VII

O thin men of Haddam[1]
Why do you imagine golden birds?
Do you not see how the blackbird
Walks around the feet
Of the women about you?

VIII

I know noble accents
And lucid, inescapable rhythms;
But I know, too,
That the blackbird is involved
In what I know.

IX

When the blackbird flew out of sight,
It marked the edge
Of one of many circles.

---

[1]City in Connecticut.

VI

The blackbird's shadow
Went back and forth, past
A big window full of
Crude glassy icicles.
The atmosphere suggested
A hidden principle
Behind that shadow.

VII

O needy men of the East Coast,
Why dream about birds made from gold?
Don't you realize that
Your womenfolk have blackbirds
Walking around their feet?

VIII

I know the blackbird
Gets into the best sounds
I know how to make:
High-flown lingos
And hot, catchy beats.

IX

When the blackbird crossed
Over the edge of my horizon
There were also lots of other horizons.

X

At the sight of blackbirds
Flying in a green light,
Even the bawds of euphony
Would cry out sharply.

XI

He rode over Connecticut
In a glass coach.
Once, a fear pierced him,
In that he mistook
The shadow of his equipage
For blackbirds.

XII

The river is moving.
The blackbird must be flying.

XIII

It was evening all afternoon.
It was snowing
And it was going to snow.
The blackbird sat
In the cedar-limbs.

X

Even the hucksters of pretty sounds
Would shout out
If they saw blackbirds
Flying among life's colors.

XI

He crossed the country
In a carriage that was all windows.
Once, he mistakenly
Thought the shadow of his luggage
Was blackbirds
Which scared him.

XII

The blackbird has to move
Because the river flows.

XIII

It was dark all afternoon.
There was snow
And going to be more.
In the evergreen limbs
There was a blackbird.

in Just-

—E. E. Cummings

in Just-
spring   when the world is mud-
luscious the little
lame balloonman

whistles   far   and wee

and eddieandbill come
running from marbles and
piracies and it's
spring

when the world is puddle-wonderful

the queer
old balloonman whistles
far   and   wee
and bettyandisbel come dancing

from hop-scotch and jump-rope and

it's
spring
and
        the
            goat-footed[1]

---

[1]Attributed to fauns, satyrs and Satan.

↻ In earliest

—de/composed from Cummings

In earliest
Spring, when the muddy world
is marvelous, the little
hunchbacked balloonman

whistles softly in the distance

then Bill and Eddie come
running from marbles and
tag games and it's
Spring

when the world is wet but wonderful.

The eccentric
old balloonman whistles
softly, far away
and Isabel and Betty come capering

from jacks and blindman's bluff and

it's
Spring
and
    the
        crippled

in Just— (continued)

balloonMan   whistles
far
and
wee

In earliest (continued)

> balloonman whistles
> softly,
> from far
> off.

anyone lived in a pretty how town

—E. E. Cummings

anyone lived in a pretty how town
(with up so floating many bells down)
spring summer autumn winter
he sang his didn't he danced his did.

Women and men(both little and small)
cared for anyone not at all
they sowed their isn't they reaped their same
sun moon stars rain

children guessed(but only a few
and down they forgot as up they grew
autumn winter spring summer)
that noone loved him more by more

when by now and tree by leaf
she laughed his joy she cried his grief
bird by snow and stir by still
anyone's any was all to her

someones married their everyones
laughed their cryings and did their dance
(sleep wake hope and then)they
said their nevers they slept their dream

stars rain sun moon
(and only the snow can begin to explain
how children are apt to forget to remember
with up so floating many bells down)

A certain man lived in a very nice town

—de/composed from Cummings

A certain man lived in a very nice town
Where bell-sounds tolled the hours and days.
While one by one the seasons passed
He sang his sorrows, he danced his joys.

Small-spirited people all around
Didn't like this man at all;
They made negations and got negations back
While spheres turned and weather changed.

Only a few of the children realized—
But they forgot as they grew up
With seasons continually passing—
That a certain woman loved him more and more.

Time passed, the trees grew
And she shared this man's emotions;
All else was antagonistic but
His concerns meant everything to her.

The rest all married somebody or other,
Disguised their feelings through life's routines,
Followed their day's course, made wishes, then
Made negative vows and forgot their ideals.

Weather changed and the spheres still turned
(And only the seasons' deaths can explain
Why children forget with passing time
The meanings they formerly knew.)

anyone lived in a pretty how town (continued)

one day anyone died i guess
(and noone stooped to kiss his face)
busy folk buried them side by side
little by little and was by was

all by all and deep by deep
and more by more they dream their sleep
noone and anyone earth by april
wish by spirit and if by yes.

Women and men(both dong and ding)
summer autumn winter spring
reaped their sowing and went their came
sun moon stars rain

A certain man lived in a very nice town (continued)

One day this man died of course
And this woman leaned down to kiss his face.
Thoughtless people buried them together—
The little couple they once had been.

Universally, profoundly,
And totally they die into their ideal,
This man and woman into new growth,
Desire into spirit and possibility into acceptance.

Others, like the sound of tolling bells,
As the seasons continued toward new growth,
Got back what they gave, left their loves
While spheres turned and weather changed.

The Drunken Fisherman

—Robert Lowell

Wallowing in this bloody sty,
I cast for fish that pleased my eye
(Truly Jehovah's bow suspends
No pots of gold to weight its ends);
Only the blood-mouthed rainbow trout
Rose to my bait. They flopped about
My canvas creel until the moth
Corrupted its unstable cloth.

A calendar to tell the day;
A handkerchief to wave away
The gnats; a couch unstuffed with storm
Pouching a bottle in one arm;
A whiskey bottle full of worms;
And bedroom slacks: are these fit terms
To mete the worm whose molten rage
Boils in the belly of old age?

Once fishing was a rabbit's foot—
O wind blow cold, O wind blow hot,
Let suns stay in or suns step out:
Life danced a jig on the sperm-whale's spout—
The fisher's fluent and obscene
Catches kept his conscience clean.
Children, the raging memory drools
Over the glory of past pools.

Fishing Drunk

—de/composed from Lowell

I wade a creek that's surging high
To cast for fish that met my eye.
Of course the rainbow's arc suspends
No pots of gold to weight its ends;
Nothing except the rainbow trout
Snapped at my bait and flopped about
Inside my creel of canvas twill
But it wore out as fabrics will.

A calendar to tell the day;
A rag to wave the gnats away;
A couch that's gone through rain and storm
And hides a bottle in one arm—
An empty whiskey fifth for bait
And bedroom slacks—no fitting state
In which to counteract the rage
That springs from passions in old age.

To fish was once my safety net—
O wind blow wild or wind blow wet,
Though suns stepped out or suns stayed in,
Life did a dance unstained by sin—
The catches that a fisher took
Kept conscience clear as any brook.
Children, I love to tell the story
Of former pools and vanished glory.

The Drunken Fisherman (continued)

Now the hot river, ebbing, hauls
Its bloody waters into holes;
A grain of sand inside my shoe
Mimics the moon that might undo
Man and Creation too; remorse,
Stinking, has puddled up its source;
Here tantrums thrash to a whale's rage.
This is the pot-hole of old age.

Is there no way to cast my hook
Out of this dynamited brook?
The Fisher's sons must cast about
When shallow waters peter out.
I will catch Christ with a greased worm,
And when the Prince of Darkness stalks
My bloodstream to its Stygian term . . .
On water the Man-Fisher walks.

Fishing Drunk (continued)

But now the muddied river rolls
Its frothing waters into holes.
A grain of sand inside my shoe
Can grate like hungers that undo
All hope of blessedness; remorse
Has soured life and fouled its source;
My angers grow to monstrous rage
Caught in the doldrums of old age.

Where else now can I cast my hook
But in the remnants of this brook?
God's children must employ their eyes
When shallow water ebbs and dies.
So then I'll just repent and pray
Whenever Death or Satan hunts
My life's course to its final day—
Salvation can be mine at once.

Dream Song #29

—John Berryman

There sat down, once, a thing on Henry's heart
só heavy, if he had a hundred years
& more, & weeping, sleepless, in all them time
Henry could not make good.
Starts again always in Henry's ears
the little cough somewhere, an odour, a chime.

And there is another thing he has in mind
like a grave Sienese face a thousand years
would fail to blur the still profiled reproach of. Ghastly,
with open eyes, he attends, blind.
All the bells say: too late. This is not for tears;
thinking.

But never did Henry, as he thought he did,
end anyone and hacks her body up
and hide the pieces, where they may be found.
He knows: he went over everyone, & nobody's missing.
Often he reckons, in the dawn, them up.
Nobody is ever missing.

↻ Dream Song #29

—de/composed from Berryman

So heavy a burden was once placed on Henry's heart
that if he lay sleepless more than a century
and wept all that time
he could not be rehabilitated.
In Henry's thoughts, there always rises
an insinuating cough, an odour, an echo.

There is another matter also in his mind
That's like a lady's classical profile whose accusations
Would go unmitigated through a thousand years. Appalled
And wide awake, he stares but can see nothing.
All things indicate this can't be rectified. Remorse is not called for;
Meditation is.

Yet Henry never did what he dreamed he'd done:
Killed somebody and destroyed their body,
Then hid the evidence which still might be discovered.
He's certain: his acquaintances are all alive and well.
In the mornings he often counts them one by one
And he has never killed anybody.

The Bundled-Well-Hung-Up-Tight-Don't-Put-That-In-Your-Mouth-It's-Poisoned-Blues

—Alice Fulton

They were always too long or too short,
too cool or stirred up
tight in her breakfast nook
maybe wired with bracelets
or loud with tattoos
& God he glistens when he moves! She held them
at arm's length, wondered what possessed
this one, narrow as a casket,
that one wearing boots with spurs, and was sure
she didn't want this
stranger holding her like some fly ball,
a fast one that happened to come
his way, she knew
she shouldn't have to
wear so many clothes
to bed, even in winter:
an embarrassment of galoshes, cowardly
macintoshes, oiled wool
sweaters, everything but
skin. Skin lived someplace else
as she let each man free
one clasp, unfasten, maybe
a buckle, a sash.

A Chaste and Cautious Song

—de/composed from Fulton

The men were all too tall or short,
too haughty or excited,
drunk, but still in her kitchen
lit up perhaps by jewelry,
flaunting tattoos
and a swaggering carriage. She observed them
from a distance, wondering what
this one—deathly thin—thought,
that one dressed Western style, and she certainly
didn't want this
interloper holding
her as if he'd caught a pop-up,
an easy one that by good luck came
his direction. She knew
she shouldn't have to
maintain so much protection
in love-making, even during barren times—
an embarrassment of put-offs, defenses,
layers of well-practiced
evasions, everything but
her unguarded self. Naked passion was banished
as she let each one disengage
one habit, possibly overcome
one pretext, one excuse.

III. The Singular Voice

Listening to unfamiliar music, we sometimes hear a style so defining that we can confidently say: this is Haydn or Mahler or Faure. Similarly, a poet's "voice" may become so distinctive that we discern not only a fictional speaker but also the actual author. Choice of subjects, ideas, or details, levels of diction, rhythm, movement, and sound textures, of imagery and allusion—these qualities may tell us that we are hearing Gerard Manley Hopkins or E. E. Cummings or John Berryman. Just as many tribal groups feel a menace—often for good reasons—from an unfamiliar dialect; many of us, fearing change or loss of power, feel threatened by a new voice in poetry. Yet individuality and novelty are particularly sought by modern artists and, just as in the sciences, have provided much richness and invention. Having got past the initial strangeness, there may be a marked pleasure in finding a once-alien voice to be familiar and reassuring.

The wide appeal of Emily Dickinson's poems clearly lies not so much in original ideas or beliefs, but in their projection of personality. The poems included here establish a seemly, almost prim, decorum which, either through shocking images, unconventional usages, or a wilful skewing of familiar stanza forms, later evolves into lines of great force. The de/compositions replace such characteristics with trite, fifth-hand effects.

In "The Oxen," as elsewhere through this collection, we recognize not only Thomas Hardy's concern with the loss of religious faith, but also his tenacious honesty in presenting complex attitudes with direct though often gnarled and countrified language. In "Drummer Hodge," the common English rural nickname (much like our "Joe" or "Chuck") confronts a foreign landscape and the alien language of South Africa during the Boer War.

Gerard Manley Hopkins, a Jesuit priest, created a style and music embodying extremes of religious exaltation or profound despair. He not only developed an eccentric prosody and markedly individual movement (which we will meet again later) but supercharged his diction with archaic or dialectic language, eccentric sentence structures, internal rhymes, alliterations, and echoes. The de/compositions tame these effects and iron out the rhythm to a common iambic norm.

Dylan Thomas's poems are equally extreme in style, though in the service of an eccentric personal pantheism. The lines of his "Refusal to Mourn . . ." (an elegy which, characteristically, claims not to be elegaic) are packed with paradoxical but grandly resounding images. In "The Force That Through the Green Fuse Drives the Flower," the main nouns and verbs are chosen both for active power, and for ambiguity of word, phrase, and sentence, underlining that the same forces drive all areas of nature. The de/composition replaces this complex animism with flat, impersonal dogma.

Hart Crane's poems, like Thomas's and many others of his period, surge beyond a late Romantic "poetic" tone into more extreme usages and an incantatory style. Echoing his own headlong pursuit of some enveloping rapture, his language consistently tends toward the esoteric, while the relation of symbol to subject is often nearly surreal. As with Thomas, however, his aim is not merely to project some prose "message content" but rather to sweep the reader up into a less conscious state of elevation.

Like Crane and Thomas in the importance of style over literal content, Robert Lowell's early poem, "The Drunken Fisherman," is surcharged with religious and literary allusions. The de/composition narrows this subject to some actual fisherman's worldly actions. Although keeping Lowell's basic meter, I have eliminated, when possible, the variations that helped charge his poem.

The work of Wallace Stevens displays a sharp contrast, taking a refined and somewhat mannered eloquence as our only hope in bringing order and symmetry to an essentially meaningless world. Fertility and beauty may well occur here but always entangled with death and inexplicable loss.

E. E. Cummings is surely one of the most recognizable of poets. Although his work retains much freshness and vigor, his influence has been so wide that readers may not realize how outrageous his poems once seemed. It is improbable that such poets as John Berryman and Alice Fulton (though we easily distinguish their voices from his) could have produced their quirky eccentricities without his example.

Berryman's "Dream Song #29," like many recent poems here, derives marked appeal from a clash between subject matter and style. Without the original's quirky song-and-dance, the poem would shrink to a sad but dreary case history. Much the same is true of Alice Fulton's "blues"—without the razzle-dazzle of her style, interest in the speaker and her suitors would evaporate. The quality of her voice, above all, certifies that she inhabits, emotionally and intellectually, a terrain which they may visit but to which they could never be naturalized.

IV

Metrics & Music

Upon Julia's Clothes

—Robert Herrick

Whenas in silks my Julia goes,
Then, then, methinks, how sweetly flows
That liquefaction of her clothes.

Next, when I cast mine eyes, and see
That brave vibration, each way free,
O, how that glittering taketh me!

Upon Julia's Garments

—de/composed from Herrick
into strict regularity

When dressed in silk my Julia goes
I always think it sweetly flows
While fluid motion sways her clothes.

When next I look at her and see
That splendid movement, loose and free,
Its gleam completely captures me!

On Kate's Gown

—de/composed from Herrick
into unmetrical lines

When in a silk dress Kate goes
How sweetly (I think) her gown flows,
Turning into liquid her clothes.

Next, looking at her, I see
That grand movement which is so free;
Her scintillation quite takes me.

Still to Be Neat

—Ben Jonson

Still[1] to be neat, still to be dressed,
As you were going to a feast;
Still to be powdered, still perfumed:
Lady, it is to be presumed,
Though art's hid causes are not found,
All is not sweet, all is not sound.

Give me a look, give me a face
That makes simplicity a grace;
Robes loosely flowing, hair as free:
Such sweet neglect more taketh me
Than all th' adulteries of art;
They strike mine eyes, but not my heart.

---

[1] Always.

Forever Neat and Dressed

—de/composed from Jonson
into iambic trimeter

Forever neatly dressed
As going to a feast,
Still powdered, still perfumed;
My lady, it's presumed
Though art's cause be not found,
Not all is sweet nor sound.

Give me a look, a face
Displaying simple grace;
Robes flowing loose, hair free
With informality;
The niceties of art
Catch eyes but miss the heart.

↻ Still Neat, Still Dressed

—de/composed from Jonson
into iambic dimeter

Still neat, still dressed
As for a feast,
Powdered, perfumed,
Miss, it's presumed,
Though no guilt's found
Yet all's not sound.

A look and face
With simple grace,
Robes loose, hair free
More pleases me;
Adulterous art
Can't strike my heart.

↻ Forever to Be Neat, Forever Dressed

—de/composed from Jonson
into iambic pentameter

Forever to be neat, forever dressed
Like someone who'll be going to a feast;
Forever to be powdered and perfumed;
My dear, I think it has to be presumed
Though such finesse may keep its cause unfound,
Not everything is sweet, not all is sound.

I much prefer a look, prefer a face
That makes of plain simplicity a grace;
Robes loosely flowing, hair that flows as free;
Such carelessness as that more taketh me
Than all the falsehoods of cosmetic art.
They strike mine eyes, but never strike my heart.

Still to Be Stylish and Evermore Dressed

—de/composed from Jonson
into anapestic tetrameter

Still to be stylish and evermore dressed
As though you were ready to go to a feast;
Still to be powdered and always perfumed;
Dear Lady, it certainly must be presumed,
Though art's hidden causes may never be found,
Not everything's sweet and not everything's sound.

So give me a look, then, and give me a face
That lets its simplicity serve as its grace;
With robes loosely flowing, hair flowing as free;
So sweet a neglect's more attractive to me
Than all the adulteries of too-stylish art;
They strike at my eyes, but can't strike at my heart.

My Picture Left in Scotland

—Ben Jonson

I now think, Love is rather deaf than blind,
          For else it could not be,
              That she,
Whom I adore so much, should so slight me,
          And cast my love behind:
I'm sure my language to her, was as sweet,
          And every close did meet
      In sentence, of as subtle feet,
          As hath the youngest He,
That sits in shadow of Apollo's tree.
Oh, but my conscious fears,
          That fly my thoughts between,
          Tell me that she hath seen
      My hundred of gray hairs,
          Told seven and forty years,
Read so much waste, as she cannot embrace
My mountain belly, and my rocky face,
And all these through her eyes, have stopped her ears.

My Photo Left in Italy

—de/composed from Jonson
into iambic tetrameter

I think that Cupid's deaf, not blind
And this opinion must be right
For otherwise my heart's delight
Would never hold my love so slight
That she would leave my gift behind.
The poetry I wrote her flows
As sweetly cadenced to its close—
Smooth-metred and well-rhymed as those
Created by the youngest blade
Beneath Apollo's tree of shade.

But O! my mind is full of fears,
That through my calmer thoughts arise
To tell me that my Lady's eyes
Have seen my myriad graying hairs
And all my forty-seven years—
More ruins than her heart can hold:
My huge paunch, wrinkled face grown old—
These fill her eyes and shut her ears.

Preludes

—T. S. Eliot

I

The winter evening settles down
With smell of steaks in passageways.
Six o'clock.
The burnt-out ends of smoky days.
And now a gusty shower wraps
The grimy scraps
Of withered leaves about your feet
And newspapers from vacant lots;
The showers beat
On broken blinds and chimney-pots,
And at the corner of the street
A lonely cab-horse steams and stamps.
And then the lighting of the lamps.

II

The morning comes to consciousness
Of faint stale smells of beer
From the sawdust-trampled street
With all its muddy feet that press
To early coffee-stands.
With the other masquerades
That time resumes,
One thinks of all the hands
That are raising dingy shades
In a thousand furnished rooms.

III

You tossed a blanket from the bed,
You lay upon your back, and waited;
You dozed, and watched the night revealing

↻ Postludes

−de/composed from Eliot

I

The winter evening settles down
With smells of steak in passageways.
The tower bell tolls six o'clock.
The ends of burnt-out smoky days
And now a gusty shower wraps
The tattered bits and withered scraps
Of last year's leaves about your feet
And papers blown from parking lots.
The chill and dirty showers beat
On window shades and chimney-pots,
While, like an image of the street,
A waiting cab-horse steams and stamps
But then they come and light the lamps.

II

The morning brings no consciousness
But only faint stale smells of beer
From off the sawdust-trampled street
With all its workmen's muddy feet
That trudge to early coffee-stands.
Besides time's other masquerades
And all our culture's false costumes
One has to think of all the hands
That now are raising window shades
Inside their bed- or living-rooms.

III

You tossed a jacket from the chair,
You sat and rocked a while, and waited;
You paced and sometimes would recall

The thousand sordid images
Of which your soul was constituted;
They flickered against the ceiling.
And when all the world came back
And the light crept up between the shutters
And you heard the sparrows in the gutters,
You had such a vision of the street
As the street hardly understands;
Sitting along the bed's edge, where
You curled the papers from your hair,
Or clasped the yellow soles of feet
In the palms of both soiled hands.

IV
His soul stretched tight across the skies
That fade behind a city block,
Or trampled by insistent feet
At four and five and six o'clock;
And short square fingers stuffing pipes,
And evening newspapers, and eyes
Assured of certain certainties,
The conscience of a blackened street
Impatient to assume the world.

. . . I am moved by fancies that are curled
Around these images, and cling:
The notion of some infinitely gentle
Infinitely suffering thing.

. . . Wipe your hand across your mouth, and laugh;
The worlds revolve like ancient women
Gathering fuel in vacant lots.

The thousand sordid memories
Of which your life was constituted;
They flickered up against the wall.
And then, when all the world came back,
And light crept up between the shutters
And you heard pigeons in the gutters,
You felt such hatred of the street
As one who's lived there understands;
You sat before your mirror, where
You brushed the tangles from your hair
Or rubbed the aching soles of feet
With both the palms of weary hands.

IV

My soul hangs, nailed across the skies
That blaze behind a city block,
Or trampled down by workmen's feet
At two and three and four o'clock;
And greasy fingers, sewer pipes
Or sandwich papers, empty eyes
In search of long-lost certainties,
The spirit of a tainted street
That yearns to dominate the world.

I am enthralled by ideals curled
Around these scenes that firmly cling:
The will to be an infinitely gentle
And infinitely suffering thing.

Just cough and spit at that, then laugh;
This world plods on like aging women
Collecting trash in parking lots.

The Sunlight on the Garden

—Louis MacNeice

The sunlight on the garden
Hardens and grows cold,
We cannot cage the minute
Within its nets of gold,
When all is told
We cannot beg for pardon.

Our freedom as free lances
Advances towards its end;
The earth compels, upon it
Sonnets and birds descend;
And soon, my friend,
We shall have no time for dances.

The sky was good for flying
Defying the church bells
And every evil iron
Siren and what it tells:
The earth compels,
We are dying, Egypt, dying

And not expecting pardon,
Hardened in heart anew,
But glad to have sat under
Thunder and rain with you,
And grateful too
For sunlight on the garden.

A Bright Day in the Garden

—de/composed from MacNeice
into unrhymed iambic trimeter

A bright day in the garden
Grows stiff and then turns chill,
We cannot cage the hour
Within the sunlight's nets;
When everything's been said
We cannot beg forgiveness.

Our freedom as free agents
Moves onward towards its end;
The earth constrains us, on it
Poems and birds will perch;
And soon, my love,
We shall have no time for dances.

The sky was good for soaring
In spite of the church bells
And every wicked brassy
Siren and what it says:
The earth constrains;
We are parting, lover, parting

Expecting no forgiveness,
Grown cold in heart again,
But glad we sat beneath
Thunder and rain together
And glad also
For bright days in the garden.

My Papa's Waltz

—Theodore Roethke

The whiskey on your breath
Could make a small boy dizzy;
But I hung on like death:
Such waltzing was not easy.

We romped until the pans
Slid from the kitchen shelf;
My mother's countenance
Could not unfrown itself.

The hand that held my wrist
Was battered on one knuckle;
At every step you missed
My right ear scraped a buckle.

You beat time on my head
With a palm caked hard by dirt,[1]
Then waltzed me off to bed
Still clinging to your shirt.

---

[1]Roethke's father was a florist and greenhouse keeper.

My Father's Dancing

—de/composed from Roethke

Your whiskey-breath smelled strong
Which turned my stomach queasy;
I had to go along
Though that was far from easy.

We stomped around; pans slid
And crashed from the kitchen shelf;
My mother frowned, then hid
And said nothing herself.

Your grip betrayed one knuckle
Bashed out of shape and queer;
Each time you lurched, your buckle
Scraped straight across my ear.

You banged time on my head,
With a fist rough as a boulder,
Then hauled me up to bed
Still hanging off your shoulder.

Father's St. Vitus' Dance

—re/de/composed from Roethke arhythmically

The whiskey that was on your breath
Made me feel dizzy;
Nevertheless, I hung on there like death:
This sort of waltz wasn't easy.

As we romped, pans
Would slide off the top shelf;
My mom's countenance
Made one unchanged frown of itself.

The hand holding my wrist
Had a bent knuckle;
Whenever a footstep was missed
My right ear got scraped on a buckle.

You beat the time on top of my head
With one palm's caked dirt,
Then waltzed me straight off to my own bed;
I, meanwhile, clung to your shirt.

Excellence

—Robert Francis

Excellence is millimeters and not miles.
From poor to good is great. From good to best is small.
From almost best to best sometimes not measurable.
The man who leaps the highest leaps perhaps an inch
Above the runner-up. How glorious the inch
And that split-second longer in the air before the fall.

○ Mastery

—de/composed from Francis
into iambic pentameter

Mastery appears in inches, not in miles.
From poor to good's great; good to best is small.
Near-best to best may be too small to measure.
He who leaps highest leaps perhaps an inch
Above the runner-up. How great that inch
And that split-second more before the fall.

To Heaven

—Ben Jonson

Good and great God, can I not think of thee,
    But it must, straight, my melancholy be?
Is it interpreted in me disease,
    That, laden with my sins, I seek for ease?
O, be thou witness, that the reins[1] dost know,
    And hearts of all, if I be sad for show,
And judge me after: if I dare pretend
    To ought but grace, or aim at other end.
As thou art all, so be thou all to me,
    First, midst, and last, converted[2] one, and three;
My faith, my hope, my love: and in this state,
    My judge, my witness, and my advocate.
Where have I been this while exil'd from thee,
    And whither rap'd,[3] now thou but stoop'st to me?
Dwell, dwell here still: O, being everywhere,
    How can I doubt to find thee ever, here?
I know my state, both full of shame, and scorn,
    Conceiv'd in sin and unto labour born,
Standing with fear, and must with horror fall,
    And destin'd unto judgement, after all.
I feel my griefs too, and there scarce is ground
    Upon my flesh t'inflict another wound.
Yet dare I not complain, or wish for death
    With holy Paul,[4] lest it be thought the breath
Of discontent; or that these prayers be
    From weariness of life, not love of thee.

---

[1] The seat of feelings.
[2] Transformed.
[3] Rapt.
[4] Cf. Romans 7:24.

Blue Heaven

—de/composed from Jonson

Almighty God! I merely think of Thee
    And straight it must my melancholy be.
Do'st Thou interpret as my soul's disease
    That, laden deep in sins, I seek for ease?
Since Thou the reins and hearts of all dost know
    Be Thou my witness if I'm sad for show;
And after judge me if I dare pretend
    To more than grace or seek some other end.
As Thou art all, be everything to me,
    The first, the midst, the last, both One and Three!
My faith, my hope, my love; despite my state,
    My judge, my witness too, and advocate.
How far away I've been, exiled from Thee
    And how transported, now Thou stoop'st to me!
So still remain! When Thou art everywhere,
    I should not doubt I'll find Thee ever here.
I know my state is full of shame and scorn:
    Conceived in sin, to heavy labour born;
I stand with fear, with horror soon to fall,
    And then must come to judgement, after all.
I feel my grief as well; there's scarcely ground
    Upon my flesh to strike another wound.
And yet I can't complain or wish for death
    For fear Thou'lt think that's discontented breath
Like holy Paul's; or think my prayers be
    From growing tired of life, not love of Thee.

The Second Coming

—William Butler Yeats

Turning and turning in the widening gyre
The falcon cannot hear the falconer;
Things fall apart; the center cannot hold;
Mere anarchy is loosed upon the world,
The blood-dimmed tide is loosed, and everywhere
The ceremony of innocence is drowned;
The best lack all conviction, while the worst
Are full of passionate intensity.

Surely some revelation is at hand;
Surely the Second Coming is at hand.
The Second Coming! Hardly are those words out
When a vast image out of *Spiritus Mundi*[1]
Troubles my sight: somewhere in sands of the desert
A shape with lion body and the head of a man,
A gaze blank and pitiless as the sun,
Is moving its slow thighs, while all about it
Reel shadows of the indignant desert birds.
The darkness drops again; but now I know
That twenty centuries of stony sleep
Were vexed to nightmare by a rocking cradle,
And what rough beast, its hour come round at last,
Slouches toward Bethlehem to be born?

---

[1]The world's soul.

Born Again

—de/composed from Yeats
into rigid regularity

From turning in its ever-widening gyre
The falcon cannot hear the falc'ner call.
Things buckle since their center cannot hold,
The violent tide is loosed and everywhere
The ritual of innocence is drowned;
The noble lack conviction, while the worst
Are full of passionate intense desire.

No doubt some revelation waits at hand;
No doubt the Second Coming's now at hand.
The Second Coming!—words I've barely said
When now an image from the spirit world
Disturbs my sight: far off in desert sands
A shape with lion trunk and human head,
A gaze that's blank and ruthless like the sun,
Is slowly moving heavy thighs; all 'round,
The shadows reel of angry desert birds.
The darkness drops again; but now I know
That twenty centuries of stony sleep
Were vexed to nightmare when a cradle rocked;
What uncouth beast, its hour come round at last
Now stalks to Bethlehem to soon be born?

They Flee from Me

—Sir Thomas Wyatt

They flee from me that sometime did me seek
With naked foot stalking in my chamber.
I have seen them, gentle, tame, and meek,
That now are wild, and do not remember
That sometime they put themself in danger
To take bread at my hand; and now they range,
Busily seeking with a continual change.

Thanked be Fortune it hath been otherwise,
Twenty times better, but once in special,
In thin array, after a pleasant guise,
When her loose gown from her shoulders did fall,
And she me caught in her arms long and small,
Therewith all sweetly did me kiss,
And softly said: "Dear heart, how like you this?"

It was no dream, I lay broad waking.
But all is turned, thorough my gentleness,
Into a strange fashion of forsaking;
And I have leave to go, of her goodness,
And she also to use newfangleness.
But since that I so kindly[1] am served,
I fain would know what she hath deserved.

---

[1]Not only "nicely" or "considerately" (here used sarcastically) but also "according to one's nature or sort"—as we would say, "What *kind* of man is he?"

The Lover Showeth How He Is Abandoned
Of Such As He Onetime Enjoyed

—Wyatt's version revised and regularized for
publication in Tottel's *Miscellany*

They flee from me, that sometime did me seek
With naked foot stalking within my chamber.
Once have I seen them, gentle, tame, and meek,
That now are wild, and do not once remember
That sometime they have put themself in danger
To take bread at my hand; and now they range,
Busily seeking in continual change.

Thanked be Fortune it hath been otherwise,
Twenty times better; but once especial,
In thin array, after a pleasant guise,
When her loose gown did from her shoulders fall,
And she me caught in her arms long and small,
And therewithal so sweetly did me kiss
And softly said, "Dear heart, how like you this?"

It was no dream, for I lay broad awaking
But all is turned now, thorough my gentleness,
Into a bitter fashion of forsaking;
And I have leave to go, of her goodness,
And she also to use newfangleness.
But since that I unkindly so am served,
How like you this? What hath she now deserved?

Now Sleeps the Crimson Petal

—Alfred, Lord Tennyson

Now sleeps the crimson petal, now the white;
Nor waves the cypress in the palace walk;
Nor winks the gold fin in the porphyry font.
The firefly wakens; waken thou with me.

Now droops the milk-white peacock like a ghost,
And like a ghost she glimmers on to me.

Now lies the Earth all Danaë to the stars,
And all thy heart lies open unto me.

Now slides the silent meteor on, and leaves
A shining furrow, as thy thoughts in me.

Now folds the lily all her sweetness up,
And slips into the bosom of the lake.
So fold thyself, my dearest, thou, and slip
Into my bosom and be lost in me.

First the Red Petals

—de/composed from Tennyson

First the red petals shut, next the white ones;
The cypress by the palace walk has quit waving;
In the stone fountain, the goldfish's fin is not winking ;
The lightning bug wakes up. So stay awake with me.

Milk white like a ghost, the peacock droops
And comes glimmering, ghost-like, in my direction.

The Earth, just like Danaë, lies under the stars
And your heart is completely open to me.

Now the inaudible meteor slides on, leaving
A bright trace, as you leave memories.

Now the lily folds its delicacy all up
And sinks into the middle of the lake;
Fold yourself up the same way, lover, and sink
Into my heart and get lost in me.

Break, Break, Break

—Alfred, Lord Tennyson

Break, break, break,
    On thy cold gray stones, O Sea!
And I would that my tongue could utter
    The thoughts that arise in me.

O, well for the fisherman's boy,
    That he shouts with his sister at play!
O, well for the sailor lad,
    That he sings in his boat on the bay!

And the stately ships go on
    To their haven under the hill;
But O for the touch of a vanished hand,
    And the sound of a voice that is still!

Break, break, break,
    At the foot of thy crags, O Sea!
But the tender grace of a day that is dead
    Will never come back to me.

Break On and On and On

—de/composed from Tennyson

Break on and on and on
        Against cold, gray stones, O Sea.
I would my tongue could tell
        The thoughts that rise in me.

It's well the fisher's boy
        Can shout with friends at play;
It's well the sailor lad
        Can sing across the bay

While stately ships sail on
        To port beneath the hill
But O to touch a vanished hand
        And hear a voice that's still.

Break on and on and on
        Below thy crags, O Sea!
The tender grace of days long dead
        Will not come back to me.

The Tyger

—William Blake

Tyger! Tyger! burning bright
In the forests of the night,
What immortal hand or eye
Could frame thy fearful symmetry?

In what distant deeps or skies
Burnt the fire of thine eyes?
On what wings dare he aspire?
What the hand, dare seize the fire?

And what shoulder, & what art,
Could twist the sinews of thy heart?
And when thy heart began to beat,
What dread hand? & what dread feet?

What the hammer? what the chain?
In what furnace was thy brain?
What the anvil? what dread grasp
Dare its deadly terrors clasp?

When the stars threw down their spears,
And water'd heaven with their tears,
Did he smile his work to see?
Did he who made the Lamb make thee?

Tyger! Tyger! burning bright
In the forests of the night,
What immortal hand or eye
Dare frame thy fearful symmetry?

↻ The Tyger

—Blake's stanzas 1 & 2
de/composed into iambics

O tyger, beast that burns so bright
In darkling forests of the night,
What godlike hand, what deathless eye
Dare frame thy fearful symmetry?

Within what distant deeps of skies
Did burn the fire of thine eyes?
Upon what wings dare he aspire?
What hand would dare to seize the fire?

↻ The Tyger

—Blake's stanzas 1 & 2
de/composed into anapests

O tyger, you creature that's burning so bright
In the threatening, darkening forests of night,
What hand of immortal, what diety's eye
Dare hope it could fashion thy feared symmetry?

Where, in the furthermost depths of the skies
Did blaze the devouring fire of thine eyes?
What are his wings that would dare to aspire?
What is the hand that would dare seize the fire?

Ah Sunflower

—William Blake

Ah Sunflower! weary of time,
Who countest the steps of the Sun,
Seeking after that sweet golden clime
Where the traveller's journey is done;

Where the Youth pined away with desire,
And the pale Virgin shrouded in snow,
Arise from their graves and aspire,
Where my Sunflower wishes to go.

↻ Ah Sunflower

—de/composed from Blake into 4' iambics

Sunflower, weary grown of time,
Who counts the footsteps of the sun
And seeks to trace that golden clime
Where every traveller's journey's done,

Where youths who pined with vain desire
And maidens shrouded white with snow
Arising from their graves, aspire
Where my sunflower yearns to go.

↻ Ah Sunflower

—de/composed from Blake into strict anapests

As the Sunflower, weary of time
Who is counting the steps of the sun
And is seeking the goldenest clime
Where the traveller's journey is done

Where the youth who had pined with desire
And the virgin all shrouded with snow
Shall arise from their graves and aspire
Where my sunflower wishes to go.

↻ Ah Sunflower

—de/composed from Blake into 3' iambics

Sunflower, tired of time,
Who counts the steps of sun
And seeks that golden clime
Where travels are all done.

Where youths pined with desire
And maidens clad with snow,
Leaving their graves, aspire
Where my flower wills to go.

Spring and Fall

To a Young Child

—Gerard Manley Hopkins

Márgarét, áre you gríeving
Over Goldengrove unleaving?
Leáves, líke the things of man, you
With your fresh thoughts care for, can you?
Áh! ás the heart grows older
It will come to such sights colder
By and by, nor spare a sigh
Though worlds of wanwood leafmeal lie;
And yet you *wíll* weep and know why.
Now no matter, child, the name:
Sórrow's spríngs áre the same.
Nor mouth had, no nor mind, expressed
What heart heard of, ghost guessed:
It ís the blight man was born for,
It is Margaret you mourn for.

Sprung and Fell

—de/composed from Hopkins

Oh Margaret, do you feel such grief
That Goldengrove falls, leaf by leaf?
Why care for leaves, with your young mind,
Instead of things of humankind?
No doubt, though, as your heart grows older
You'll surely come to such sights colder
When time has passed and you won't care
If dead leaves scatter everywhere.
You'll weep, though, when you're more aware:
Don't trouble now about the name;
The springs of sorrow are the same.
Although no mouth or mind expressed
What your heart heard, your spirit guessed.
For such a blight mankind was born;
It's Margaret that you can't help mourn.

Heaven-Haven

(a nun takes the veil)

—Gerard Manley Hopkins

I have desired to go
　　Where springs not fail,
To fields where flies no sharp and sided hail
　　And a few lilies blow.

And I have asked to be
　　Where no storms come,
Where the green swell is in the havens dumb,
　　And out of the swing of the sea.

⟳ Paradise-Refuge

(a nun takes the veil)

—de/composed from Hopkins

I'd like to go
　　Where springs don't ever fail,
To fields without any flying, sharp-sided hail,
　　And a small number of lilies blow.

I've requested to be
　　Where storms don't come,
To havens in which green breakers are dumb
　　And aren't swung by the sea.

Rest

—Hopkins's first version

I have desired to go
    Where springs not fail;
To fields where flies not the unbridled hail,
    And a few lilies blow

I have desired to be
    Where havens are dumb;
Where the green water-heads may never come,
    And in the unloved sea.

The Leaden Echo and the Golden Echo

Maidens' Song from St. Winefred's Well

—Gerard Manley Hopkins

THE LEADEN ECHO

How to kéep—is there ány any, is there none such, nowhere known
    some, bow or brooch or braid or brace, láce, latch or catch or key
    to keep
Back beauty, keep it, beauty, beauty, beauty, . . . from vanishing
    away?
Ó is there no frowning of these wrinkles, rankèd wrinkles deep,
Dówn? no waving off of these most mournful messengers, still messen-
    gers, sad and stealing messengers of grey?
No there's none, there's none, O no there's none,
Nor can you long be, what you now are, called fair,
Do what you may do, what, do what you may,
And wisdom is early to despair:
Be beginning; since no, nothing can be done
To keep at bay
Age and age's evils, hoar hair,
Ruck and wrinkle, drooping, dying, death's worst, winding-
    sheets, tombs and worms and tumbling to decay;
So be beginning, be beginning to despair.
O there's none; no no no there's none:
Be beginning to despair; to despair,
Despair, despair, despair, despair.

The Leaden Echo and the Golden Echo

Maidens' Song from St. Winefred's Well

—de/composed from Hopkins

THE LEADEN ECHO

Isn't there any known method or attachment to prevent

Beauty from departing?
Some way to repel these lined creases

And drive off these creeping, mournful, inaudible heralds of old age?

No there isn't
And you can't be attractive for very long
Whatever you do.
So it's smart to feel despondent soon
Or right now since there's no way
To block out
Ageing's troubles, gray hair,
Wrinkles, sagging, morbidity, death's horrors, shrouds, graves, maggots
    and rotting;
Start abandoning hope.
There's no answer
So begin to lose heart,
Give up and despair.

The Leaden Echo and the Golden Echo (continued)

THE GOLDEN ECHO

  Spare!

There ís one, yes I have one (Hush there!);

Only not within seeing of the sun,

Not within the singeing of the strong sun,

Tall sun's tingeing, or treacherous the tainting of the earth's air,

Somewhere elsewhere there is ah well where! one,

Oñe. Yes I cán tell such a key, I dó know such a place,

Where whatever's prized and passes of us, everything that's fresh and
    fast flying of us, seems to us sweet of us and swiftly away with,
    done away with, undone,

Úndone, done with, soon done with, and yet dearly and dangerously
    sweet

Of us, the wimpled-water-dimpled, not-by-morning-matchèd face,

The flower of beauty, fleece of beauty, too too apt to, ah! to fleet,

Never fleets móre, fastened with the tenderest truth

To its own best being and its loveliness of youth: it is an everlasting-
    ness of, O it is an all youth!

Come then, your ways and airs and looks, locks, maiden gear, gallantry
    and gaiety and grace,

Winning ways, airs innocent, maiden manners, sweet looks, loose locks,
    long locks, lovelocks, gaygear, going gallant, girlgrace—

Resign them, sign them, seal them, send them, motion them with
    breath,

And with sighs soaring, soaring síghs, deliver

Them; beauty-in-the-ghost, deliver it, early now, long before death

Give beauty back, beauty, beauty, beauty, back to God, beauty's self
    and beauty's giver.

See: not a hair is, not an eyelash, not the least lash lost; every hair

Is, hair of the head, numbered.

THE GOLDEN ECHO

Stop that!
I have one, so be quiet.
But not in the sun's range of sight
Or of its burning
Which contaminates earth's atmosphere;
Some place, though not here, there exists
A solution. I know the clue and the place
Where whatever we value as new and lovely though quickly obliterated,

Wiped out though precariously beautiful,

The face veiled like pock-marked water, more splendid than dawn's light,
The bloom and curl of good looks, only too short-lived,
Never leaves, since it's bound with real compassion
To its full nature and young prettiness; it is eternal youth!

Come, your behavior and appearance, hairdo, fashions and cheerful
    elegance,
Appealing maiden ways, innocent charm, coy glances, loosened hair,
    fancy fashions, dashing style, female grace,
Yield, pack and send them with your breath

And with hovering sighs,
Long before death hand over up the soul's beauty
To God, beauty's essence and bestower.

See: not one hair or smallest eyelash gets lost; each one
Has been counted.

The Leaden Echo and the Golden Echo (continued)

Nay, what we had lighthanded left in surly the mere mould
Will have waked and have waxed and walked with the wind
　　what while we slept,
This side, that side hurling a heavyheaded hundredfold
What while we, while we slumbered.
O then, weary then whý should we tread? O why are we so haggard
　　at the heart, so care-coiled, care-killed, so fagged, so fashed, so
　　cogged, so cumbered,
When the thing we freely fórfeit is kept with fonder a care,
Fonder a care kept than we could have kept it, kept
Far with fonder a care (and we, we should have lost it) finer,
　　fonder
A care kept.—Where kept? Do but tell us where kept, where.—
Yonder.—What high as that! We follow, now we follow.—Yonder,
　　yes yonder, yonder,
Yonder.

Indeed, the seed we casually sprinkled on rough ground
Will have sprouted, grown and waved in the breeze

Throwing its myriad heads to this side and that
While we just slept.
Then why do we trudge with tired hearts, troubled, worn to exhaustion
  and death by our burdens

When what we freely hand over is preserved with more thoughtfulness
Than we could give it and is maintained
Far off more carefully, though we would have lost it.—

But where, just tell us that.—
Over there.—That high? Then we follow.—Yes,

Let's go over there.

Cavalry Crossing a Ford

—Walt Whitman

A line in long array where they wind betwixt green islands,
They take a serpentine course, their arms flash in the sun—hark to the
    musical clank,
Behold the silvery river, in it the splashing horses loitering stop to drink,
Behold the brown-faced men, each group, each person a picture, the
    negligent rest on the saddles,
Some emerge on the opposite bank, others are just entering the ford—while,
Scarlet and blue and snowy white,
The guidon[1] flags flutter gayly in the wind.

---

[1] A small pennant carried by a military unit.

Cavalry Crossing a Ford

—de/composed from Whitman

A long, stretched-out line, winding through islands of greenery,
Their course curves snakelike, in the sunlight their arms flash—listen to
    the musical clanking,
The river is silvery, the horses splash, loiter and drink,
The men have brown faces, each group or person forming a picture, some
    negligently resting on the saddles,
Some leave at the far bank, some are just now entering the ford,
And meanwhile, snowy white, blue and scarlet,
In the wind the guidon flags gayly flutter.

Bivouac on a Mountain Side

—Walt Whitman

I see before me now a traveling army halting,
Below a fertile valley spread, with barns and the orchards of summer,
Behind, the terraced sides of a mountain, abrupt, in places rising high,
Broken, with rocks, with clinging cedars, with tall shapes dingily seen,
The numerous camp-fires scatter'd near and far, some away up on the
    mountain,
The shadowy forms of men and horses, looming, large-sized, flickering,
And over all the sky—the sky! far, far out of reach, studded, breaking out, the
    eternal stars.

Bivouac on a Mountain Side

—de/composed from Whitman

I now see an army halted on its march;
A valley with barns and fertile summer orchards below them;
Behind, terraced mountain sides, abruptly rising in places,
Interspersed by rocks or clinging cedars or large, dingy shapes,
Many campfires randomly here and there, some of them very high up on
    the mountain peaks,
Shadows of both horses and men that loom, huge, aflicker,
And above everything else, the sky!—too distant to grasp, with studs
    working their way through, the stars that endure forever.

Tears

—Walt Whitman

Tears! tears! tears!
In the night, in solitude, tears,
On the white shore dripping, dripping, suck'd in by the sand,
Tears, not a star shining, all dark and desolate,
Moist tears from the eyes of a muffled head;
O who is that ghost? that form in the dark, with tears?
What shapeless lump is that, bent, crouch'd there on the sand?
Streaming tears, sobbing tears, throes, choked with wild cries;
O storm, embodied, rising, careering with swift steps along the beach!
O wild and dismal night storm, with wind—O belching and desperate!
O shade so sedate and decorous by day, with calm countenance and regulated
    pace,
But away at night, as you fly, none looking—O then the unloosen'd ocean,
Of tears! tears! tears!

↻ Weeping

—de/composed from Whitman

Weeping, more and more weeping!
Nightly, when all alone, still more weeping;
Dripping onto the white shore, dripping for the sand to suck in;
Weeping, the stars are not out, everything's desolate and dark;
Moisture of tears from a muffled head's eyes:
O what ghost is that? in darkness what weeping form?
What vague mound is that, bowed to the sand, crouched down?
Weeping in streams, sobbing—choked with shrieks;
Materialized storm, growing, rushing, hurtling along the beach!
O violent, grim, nocturnal tempest! O outbursting and wild!
O spirit composed and proper by daylight, with calm expression and with
    steady footsteps,
But at night, no one watching, away you fly—O then the high seas
Of weeping, more and more weeping.

The Main Deep

—James Stephens

The long, rolling,
Steady-pouring,
Deep-trenchèd
Green billow:

The wide-topped,
Unbroken,
Green-glacid,
Slow-sliding,

Cold-flushing,
On—on—on—
Chill-rushing,
Hush-hushing,

Hush-hushing. . . .

An Ocean Wave

—de/composed from Stephens

Outstretched, the flowing
Wave pours constantly
Between its deep troughs
Green and billowy:

Broad at the top,
Without interruption,
Glacially green,
It slowly slides

Coldly surging
Onward continually
To break icily,
Then quietly ebbing,

Wanes in silence.

Bethsabe's Song

—George Peele

Hot sun, cool fire, tempered with sweet air,
Black shade, fair nurse, shadow my white hair:
Shine, sun; burn, fire; breathe, air, and ease me;
Black shade, fair nurse, shroud me and please me:
Shadow, my sweet nurse, keep me from burning,
Make not my glad cause cause of mourning.
     Let not my beauty's fire
     Inflame unstaid desire,
     Nor pierce any bright eye
     That wandereth lightly.

Bathsheba's Song

—de/composed from Peele

The sun is hot but its fire is cool if tempered by sweet air
So shade my hair, black shadow, sweet nurse of mine;
Sun, keep on shining; fire, burn on, but blow, air, and soothe me;
Dark shade, my careful nurse, shroud and comfort me;
Shadow, protect me as a kindly nurse, from burning;
Do not let my blithe aims lead to sorrow.

> Do not let my beauty's fire
> Stir up lewd desire
> Nor pierce some shifty eye
> That's prowling lightly.

The Return

—Ezra Pound

See, they return; ah, see the tentative
    Movements, and the slow feet,
    The trouble in the pace and the uncertain
    Wavering!

See, they return, one, and by one,
With fear, as half-awakened;
As if the snow should hesitate
And murmur in the wind,
      and half turn back;
These were the "Wing'd-with-Awe,"
    Inviolable.

Gods of the wingèd shoe!
With them the silver hounds,
      sniffing the trace of air!

Haie! Haie!
    These were the swift to harry;
These the keen-scented;
These were the souls of blood.

Slow on the leash,
      pallid the leash-men!

Coming Back

—de/composed from Pound

Look at that, they're coming back; just look
    At the vague moves and the sluggish feet
    The defective pace and the lack
    Of convinced purpose.

Separately, they're coming back,
Fearful, as if only partially waked up
Or like flakes of snow that hesitate
Quietly muttering in the wind
      and partially turning back.
Others called them "The Swift and Terrible"
      Not to be resisted.

Gods whose ankles have wings!
Hounds of silver went with them
     hot on the scent!

Onward! Onward!
   They attacked swiftly,
They had sensitive noses,
Their souls were keen for blood.

They slowly walk on short leashes,
     pale men on a leash!

↻ Limping Home

—de/composition from Pound into prose

See, they return; ah, see the tentative movements, and the slow feet; the trouble in the pace and the uncertain wavering! See, they return, one, and by one, with fear, as half-awakened; as if the snow should hesitate and murmur in the wind, and half turn back.

These were the "Wing'd with Awe." Inviolable. Gods of the wingèd shoe! With them the silver hounds, sniffing the trace of air! Haie! Haie! These were the swift to harry; these the keen-scented; these were the souls of blood.

Slow on the leash, pallid the leash-men!

In a Station of the Metro

— Ezra Pound

The apparition of these faces in the crowd;
Petals on a wet, black bough.

↻ In a Subway Passage

— Abstract de/composition from Pound

The vision of these faces among the crowd
bringing beauty into a dark, forbidding scene.

↻ In an Abandoned Subway Tunnel

— Urban Realism de/composition from Pound

The sudden appearance of this crowd of faces,
Used condoms flushing down a muddy sewer.

↻ At the Garden Party

— Hallmark Version

The flushed appearance of these faces from our set,
Pink peonies on a dark green bough.

↻ Helter-Skelter Street Scene

— Nonmetrical de/composition from Pound

Among the crowds, a spectre—these faces:
Petals on a branch, all wet and black.

No Swan so Fine

—Marianne Moore

"No water so still as the
      dead fountains of Versailles." No swan,
with swart blind look askance
and gondoliering legs, so fine
      as the chintz china one with fawn-
brown eyes and toothed gold
collar on to show whose bird it was.

Lodged in the Louis Fifteenth
      candelabrum-tree of cockscomb-
tinted buttons, dahlias,
sea urchins, and everlastings,
      it perches on the branching foam
of polished sculptured
flowers—at ease and tall. The king is dead.

No Swan so Fine

—de/composed from Moore
(changes given in italics)

"No water so still as the
    dead fountains of Versailles." No swan,
with swart blind look askance
and with *black, paddling* legs, so fine
    As this *china swan, its eyes fawn-*
brown and its toothed collar
of gold telling who once owned the bird.

Lodged in the *Eighteenth Century*
    candelabrum-tree of scarlet-
tinted buttons, dahlias,
sea urchins and *chrysanthemums,*
    it perches on the branching jet
of polished, sculptured
flowers, *though the king has passed away.*

The Mind is an Enchanting Thing

—Marianne Moore

is an enchanted thing
        like the glaze on a
katydid-wing
           subdivided by sun
           till the nettings are legion.
Like Gieseking[1] playing Scarlatti;

like the apteryx-awl
        as a beak, or the
kiwi's rain-shawl
          of haired feathers, the mind
          feeling its way as though blind,
walks along with its eyes on the ground.

It has memory's ear
        that can hear without
having to hear.
          Like the gyroscope's fall,
          truly unequivocal
because trued by regnant certainty,

it is a power of
        strong enchantment. It
is like the dove-
          neck animated by
          sun; it is memory's eye;
it's conscientious inconsistency.

---

[1] German piano virtuoso.

The Mind Is Both

—de/composed from Moore

enchanting and enchanted
        like the patina on the wing
of a katydid
           which the sun splits
           into multiple networks.
Like Scarlatti performed by Gieseking;

like the awl-shaped
        beak of a kiwi
or its raincape
           of hairy feathers, the mind
           as though sightless
feels its way along with its eyes down.

It has the ear of memory
        that can function without
having to function.
           Like a falling gyroscope,
           completely unconditional
since controlled by absolute principles,

it is a force
        of powerful magic. It
is like the neck
           of a dove invigorated by
           sunlight, it is memory's vision;
it is conscientious about being inconsistent.

The Mind is an Enchanting Thing (continued)

It tears off the veil; tears
       the temptation, the
mist the heart wears,
          from its eyes,—if the heart
          has a face; it takes apart
dejection. It's fire in the dove-neck's

iridescence; in the
         inconsistencies
of Scarlatti.
         Unconfusion submits
         its confusion to proof; it's
not a Herod's oath that cannot change.

The Mind Is Both (continued)

It removes the mask, removes
      the false charm, the
illusion our emotions create
        before their own eyes,—if emotions
        have a face; it analyzes
depression. It's vitality in the dove-neck's

opalescence, in
      Scarlatti's
deviations.
        Certainty offers
        its confusion to proof; it's
not a tyrant's word which is immutable.

Bagpipe Music

—Louis MacNeice

It's no go the merrygoround, it's no go the rickshaw,
All we want is a limousine and a ticket for the peepshow.
Their knickers are made of crêpe-de-chine, their shoes are made of python,
Their halls are lined with tiger rugs and their walls with heads of bison.

John MacDonald found a corpse, put it under the sofa,
Waited till it came to life and hit it with a poker,
Sold its eyes for souvenirs, sold its blood for whiskey,
Kept its bones for dumb-bells to use when he was fifty.

It's no go the Yogi-Man, it's no go Blavatsky,[1]
All we want is a bank balance and a bit of skirt in a taxi.

Annie MacDougall went to milk, caught her foot in the heather,
Woke to hear a dance record playing of Old Vienna.
It's no go your maidenheads, it's no go your culture,
All we want is a Dunlop tyre and the devil mend the puncture.

The Laird o' Phelps spent Hogmanay[2] declaring he was sober,
Counted his feet to prove the fact and found he was one foot over.
Mrs. Carmichael had her fifth, looked at the job with repulsion,
Said to the midwife "Take it away; I'm through with over-production."

It's no go the gossip column, it's no go the ceilidh,[3]
All we want is a mother's help and a sugar-stick for the baby.

---

[1] Madame Blavatsky: cultish leader and author.
[2] Scottish: New Year's Eve.
[3] Scottish social gathering.

Celtic Tune

—de/composed from MacNeice

Merrygorounds are no use; neither are rickshaws;
We want a limousine and tickets for the burlesque.
Some have lightweight silk trousers and snakeskin shoes;
Tiger rugs line their chambers; the walls have bison heads.

Finding a body, John MacDonald stuffed it under his couch;
It revived so he hit it with fire tongs,
Selling its eyes for keepsakes and its blood for cognac,
Keeping its bones for weight-lifting when he gets old.

Neither Oriental priests will help out nor Western gurus;
We want a checking account and a girl in the backseat.

Going milking, Annie MacDougall slipped on the heather
And woke up listening to a recording of old waltzes.
Virginity won't do; the fine arts won't either;
We want comfortable tires and to hell with nail holes.

On New Year's Eve, the Lord of Phelps claimed he wasn't drunk,
Counted his feet for proof and got three.
Mrs. Carmichael bore her fifth baby and was repelled by it—
Said to the midwife, "Keep that; I've got too many now."

Publicity won't do, neither will dance parties,
We want nursemaids and pacifiers for the baby.

Bagpipe Music (continued)

Willie Murray cut his thumb, couldn't count the damage,
Took the hide of an Ayrshire cow and used it for a bandage.
His brother caught three hundred cran[4] when the seas were lavish,
Threw the bleeders back in the sea and went upon the parish.

It's no go the Herring Board, it's no go the Bible,
All we want is a packet of fags when our hands are idle.

It's no go the picture palace, it's no go the stadium,
It's no go the country cot with a pot of pink geraniums,
It's no go the Government grants, it's no go the elections,
Sit on your arse for fifty years and hang your hat on a pension.

It's no go my honey love, it's no go my poppet;
Work your hands from day to day, the winds will blow the profit.
The glass is falling hour by hour, the glass will fall for ever,
But if you break the bloody glass you won't hold up the weather.

---

[4]Herring.

Celtic Tune (continued)

Willie Murray cut his thumb; couldn't judge the injury;
Took an Ayrshire cow's hide to wrap up the wound.
His brother caught lots of herring when seas were full,
Threw them all back in the sea and went on welfare.

Forget the Fisheries Committee; forget the holy books;
We want a cigarette pack when we've nothing to do.

Movie houses won't help you; the same for ball parks,
Neither will rustic bungalows with pots of flowers;
Government grants won't help you; neither will voting booths;
Sit around idle for a half century, then take retirement.

It makes no sense, sweetie pie; makes no sense, baby;
Work like a dog every day and you still lose out.
The gauges fall every hour and will to the end of time
But scrapping the gauges won't halt the elements.

Musée des Beaux Arts

—W. H. Auden

About suffering they were never wrong,
The Old Masters: how well they understood
Its human position; how it takes place
While someone else is eating or opening a window or just walking dully along;
How, when the aged are reverently, passionately waiting
For the miraculous birth, there always must be
Children who did not specially want it to happen, skating
On a pond at the edge of the wood:
They never forgot
That even the dreadful martyrdom must run its course
Anyhow in a corner, some untidy spot
Where the dogs go on with their doggy life and the torturer's horse
Scratches its innocent behind on a tree.

In Brueghel's *Icarus,* for instance: how everything turns away
Quite leisurely from the disaster; the ploughman may
Have heard the splash, the forsaken cry,
But for him it was not an important failure; the sun shone
As it had to on the white legs disappearing into the green
Water; and the expensive delicate ship that must have seen
Something amazing, a boy falling out of the sky,
Had somewhere to get to and sailed calmly on.

Musée des Mals Arts

—de/composed from Auden

How well they comprehended, the Old Masters,
The situation of Mankind's disasters,
Which come to pass while others eat and talk,
Open the windows or just dully walk;
How when the old are reverently waiting
For Jesus' birth, there must be children skating
Upon a pond beside a frozen wood—
Children who thought the change might not be good.
Further, Old Masters always understood
That martyrdom and torture like as not
Take place in some ill-lighted, cluttered spot
Where beasts endure their troubles, try to ease
Their ills and quite ignore men's agonies.

In Brueghel's *Icarus,* all things turn away
From the catastrophe: the ploughman may
Have heard the splash and the forsaken cry
But didn't really care; the sun on high
Still lit those legs that fell into the green
Bay water while the ship that must have seen—
How strange! a person plunging from the sky—
Needing to get someplace, sailed calmly by.

Song of the Old Soldier

—W. H. Auden

When the Sex War ended with the slaughter of the Grandmothers,
They found a bachelor's baby suffocating under them;
Somebody called him George and that was the end of it;
    They hitched him up to the Army.
    George, you old debutante,
    How did you get in the Army?

In the Retreat from Reason he deserted on his rocking-horse
And lived on a fairy's kindness till he tired of kicking her;
He smashed her spectacles and stole her check-book and mackintosh
    Then cruised his way back to the Army.
    George, you old numero,
    How did you get in the Army?

Before the Diet of Sugar he was using razor-blades
And exited soon after with an allergy to maidenheads;
He discovered a cure of his own, but no one would patent it,
    So he showed up again in the Army.
    George, you old flybynight,
    How did you get in the Army?

When the Vice Crusades were over he was hired by some Muscovites
Prospecting for deodorants among the Eskimos;
He was caught by a common cold and condemned to the whiskey mines,
    But schlemozzled back to the Army.
    George, you old Emperor,
    How did you get in the Army?

The Old Soldier

—de/composed from Auden

When wars between the sexes stopped, all older folks were shot;
They found an orphan baby half-dead underneath the lot
So someone called the creature George—the only name it got—
    And sent it to the Army.
    George, you raw recruit,
    You're a soldier now.

When we withdrew from common sense, he fled by rocking horse
And then sponged off a kindly soul, but kicked her in the arse,
Shattered her glasses, stole her coat, then made off with her purse
    And wandered back to his outfit.
    You're a nonentity, Mister,
    This is military life.

Until euphoria'd been established, George used razor blades
But soon evolved a great disgust for virginal, pure maids;
The way he found a way to alter that brought George few accolades
    So he reappeared in uniform.
    You're a slippery devil, George,
    Who let you re-enlist?

After the Vice Squads went away, some Russians paid him well
To seek among the Eskimos some way to change men's smell
But with sick complaints and gin mills he turned that life a hell
    And slunk back into the ranks.
    It's that habitual loser, George,
    Back in the service once again.

Song of the Old Soldier (continued)

Since Peace was signed with Honour he's been minding his business;
But, whoops, here comes His Idleness, buttoning his uniform;
Just in time to massacre the Innocents;
    He's come home to roost in the Army.
    George, you old matador,
    Welcome back to the Army.

The Old Soldier (continued)

Since Peace (they said) was signed with Honour, he's shown diligence
Yet here he comes, the idle lout, pulling on khaki pants
In time to join the Massacre of all the Innocents.
    He's signed on for the full career.
    As a veteran killer, George,
    Glad to see you again.

Queen-Anne's-Lace

—William Carlos Williams

Her body is not so white as
anemone petals nor so smooth—nor
so remote a thing. It is a field
of the wild carrot taking
the field by force; the grass
does not rise above it.
Here is no question of whiteness,
white as can be, with a purple mole
at the center of each flower.
Each flower is a hand's span
of her whiteness. Wherever
his hand has lain there is
a tiny purple blemish. Each part
is a blossom under his touch
to which the fibres of her being
stem one by one, each to its end,
until the whole field is a
white desire, empty, a single stem,
a cluster, flower by flower,
a pious wish to whiteness gone over—
or nothing.

↻ Wild Carrot

—de/composed from Williams

Her body's not so white as anemone petals
nor so smooth—
nor so remote a thing.

It is a field of the wild carrot
taking the field by force.
The grass does not rise above it.
Here is no question of whiteness,
white as can be with a purple mole
at the center of each flower.
Each flower
is a hand's span of her whiteness.
Wherever his hand has lain
there is a tiny purple blemish.
Each part is a blossom under his touch
to which the fibres of her being stem
one by one, each to its end,
until the whole field is a white desire,
empty, a single stem,
a cluster, flower by flower,
a pious wish to whiteness gone over—
or nothing.

↻ Queen-Anne's-Lace

—de/composed from Williams into prose

Her body's not so white as anemone petals nor so smooth—nor
so remote a thing. It is a field of the wild carrot taking the field by
force. The grass does not rise above it. Here is no question of
whiteness, white as can be with a purple mole at the center of each
flower. Each flower is a hand's span of her whiteness. Wherever his
hand has lain there is a tiny purple blemish. Each part is a blossom
under his touch to which the fibres of her being stem one by one,
each to its end, until the whole field is a white desire, empty, a
single stem, a cluster, flower by flower, a pious wish to whiteness
gone over—or nothing.

Spring and All

-William Carlos Williams

By the road to the contagious hospital
under the surge of the blue
mottled clouds driven from the
northeast—a cold wind. Beyond, the
waste of broad, muddy fields
brown with dried weeds, standing and fallen

patches of standing water
and scattering of tall trees

All along the road the reddish
purplish, forked, upstanding, twiggy
stuff of bushes and small trees
with dead, brown leaves under them
leafless vines—

Lifeless in appearance, sluggish
dazed spring approaches—

They enter the new world naked,
cold, uncertain of all
save that they enter. All about them
the cold, familiar wind—

Now the grass, tomorrow
the stiff curl of wildcarrot leaf
One by one objects are defined—
It quickens: clarity, outline of leaf

Spring and All

— de/composed from Williams

By the road to the contagious hospital
under the surge of the blue mottled clouds
driven from the northeast—
a cold wind.
Beyond, the waste of broad, muddy fields
brown with dried weeds standing

and fallen patches of standing water
and scattering of tall trees

All along the road
the reddish, purplish, forked, upstanding, twiggy stuff
of bushes and small trees
with dead, brown leaves under them,
lifeless vines.

Lifeless in appearance, sluggish—
dazed spring approaches.

They enter the world, naked, cold,
uncertain of all
save that they enter.
All about them, the cold, familiar wind.

Now the grass,
tomorrow the stiff curl of wildcarrot leaf
One by one objects are defined—
It quickens: clarity, outline of leaf.

Spring and All (continued)

But now the stark dignity of
entrance—Still, the profound change
has come upon them: rooted, they
grip down and begin to awaken.

Spring and All (continued)

But now the stark dignity of entrance—
Still, the profound change has come upon them:
rooted, they grip down
and begin to awaken.

Poem

—William Carlos Williams

As the cat
climbed over
the top of

the jamcloset
first the right
forefoot

carefully
then the hind
stepped down

into the pit of
the empty
flowerpot

↻ Poetry

—de/composed from Williams

As the cat climbed
over the top
of the jamcloset

first
the right forefoot
carefully

then the hind
stepped down

into the pit
of the empty flowerpot

↻ (Prose Poem)

—de/composed by Michael Meyer

As the cat climbed over the top of the jamcloset, first the right forefoot carefully then the hind stepped down into the pit of the empty flowerpot.

IV. Metrics & Music

"Talk like rain, Missy!" That was how, Isak Dinesen tells us, the native workers on her drought-stricken African farm asked her to recite poems for them. And for many centuries, our poetry has moved in rainlike sounds, as if in the veils of some ceremony, steadily promising some undefined harvest and fulfillment.

A high percentage of English verse is written in iambic measure, which organizes the natural tendency of English to sprinkle one or two light syllables in between the heavier, more meaningful, accented ones. Since, in accenting them, we usually hold these more meaningful syllables for longer, we also tend to create a rhythm somewhat comparable to that of our music. This often helps to extend poetry's range into less conscious areas of mind, yet such strict alternation, if long continued, can grow deadening and weary. Thus, we have developed a wide range of variations that offer rhythmic and dramatic possibilities of expression.

Robert Herrick's "Upon Julia's Clothes" builds on a base of iambic tetrameter: four accents per line, each preceded by one light, unaccented syllable. I have reduced this, first, to a numbing regularity; the second de/composition keeps Herrick's syllable count but breaks the syntax and displaces accents—the awkward rhythm suggests neither Julia's graceful motions nor the speaker's fascination.

Ben Jonson's "Still to Be Neat" was considered in Section I; here I've de/composed it either into shorter lines (first trimeter, having three feet or accents, then into dimeter with only two) or else into the longer pentameter lines (five feet each), and finally into anapests, which add extra light syllables between accents. The earlier versions are cramped and overpacked; the later ones padded and/or senselessly rollicking. Meter and meaning, then, are closely involved; we cannot afford to slight either the conscious prose sense or the "mood music" of poetic rhythms. Yet, if translated to another language, all these versions would yield nearly the same meaning. Jonson's "My Picture Left in Scotland" varies the iambic meter with different line lengths and by packing heavier stresses into areas of special meaning and feeling, letting other phrases move lightly and rapidly. Thus the meter, though unbroken, is syncopated, flexible, and renders Jonson's disillusionment with wry wit. Robert Pinsky has noted that to Londoners of Jonson's time, Scotland seemed a mountainous, rocky semiwaste; one's picture, necessarily hand-painted, would have been a very special gift.

"Preludes" by T. S. Eliot is also based on iambic tetrameter, and similarly permits itself extra or movable stresses and varying line lengths, so producing a sinuous muscularity absent from the regularized and padded de/composition. This is most notable in the early sections; later, I have torn down other excellences as well.

Louis MacNeice's "The Sunlight on the Garden" uses the tricky iambic trimeter and adds a multiplicity of feminine (two-syllable) rhymes. This might have produced either an overly precious music or a feeling of virtuoso display; here, it yields a sense of grace and graciousness to a regretful parting of lovers and the probable approach of war.

A student once observed that Roethke's "My Papa's Waltz" has a "waltzing rhythm." This is suggested both by the poem's subject and by the iambic meter that usually produces a triple (3/4 or 3/8) rhythm. Roethke's skillful variations of stress as well as his slanted rhymes (dizzy/easy, pans/counte-nance) give his waltz a slightly tipsy feeling. My first de/composition changes the emotional coloring of the interplay between father and son, though it maintains the rhythm; the second keeps, when possible, the original's chief nouns and verbs but drives out any suggestion of rhythmic movement.

Robert Francis's "Excellence" takes the iambic norm to a longer than usual length: six feet per line, with a seventh foot for the last line's extra "split-second." Here, a meter which could easily seem plodding feels conversational but precise; the de/composition, homogenized into pentameter, is not even a "runner-up" to Francis's "excellence."

Jonson's moving prayer, "To Heaven," uses the pentameter line of five feet—our most common measure because of its combination of weight and flexibility. Less conspicuously musical, it is well suited to serious contemplation or speech. Cramping it into strict regularity, I have dissolved Jonson's passion and anguished questioning.

In "The Second Coming," William Butler Yeats not only handles accents with the same freedoms found in Jonson—inverted feet, spondees and pyrrhic feet—but also with extra light syllables between stresses. As usual, I have leveled and flattened this powerful vision.

For many years, we knew Sir Thomas Wyatt's poems only in versions which had been deliberately corrupted to conform to the "smoothness" (i.e., strict alternation of stress and nonstress) preferred by a later generation. In the 1920s, however, his original manuscripts were discovered in the British Museum; his freer, more expressive rhythms came to have a strong influence on contemporary poets.

Alfred, Lord Tennyson's "Now Sleeps the Crimson Petal" displays qualities familiar in many Romantic and Victorian poems: "poetic" subject matter, archaic diction and syntax, heavily sonorous vowel sounds. Tennyson creates, despite the style's limitations, an alluring music—as witnessed by the poem's many settings by song composers. He is no less skillful in the "accentual" or "stress" verse we associate with folk poetry and which counts only the main heavy beats of each line, allowing light syllables to dispose themselves at random. In "Break, Break, Break," this freedom lets him build a climactic sense of outrage against those who do not share his sense of loss.

William Blake's famous "The Tyger" is composed in trochaic tetrameter, evoking an ominous, spellbound quality unmatchable in other meters. In "Ah Sunflower" Blake uses the so-called "triple meters," anapests and dactyls, which for many others have yielded a brain-deadening "bounce." Blake, however cannily manages extra and secondary stresses to maintain but vary this rhythm.

Writing during Tennyson's ascendancy, Gerard Manley Hopkins, a Jesuit priest, also felt driven to find more individual variants of the standard prosodies. Although he was published only after his death, his "sprung rhythm" has come to have great influence among contemporary poets and critics. In "Spring and Fall," he takes new and greater liberties with the tetrameter line and with diction and syntax. His eccentric rhetoric and music provide an individuality entirely lost by my regimentation. A similar rhythm and music are found in "Heaven-Haven"; the earlier version points to his deliberate search for this idiosyncratic technique to balance against his commonplace message. Although Hopkins described "The Leaden Echo and the Golden Echo" (a choral poem from his unfinished play *St. Winefred's Well*) as "sprung rhythm," his freedom of line length as well as syllable and stress count, suggest rhymed (though astonishingly rhythmical) free verse. Hopkins even supplies diacritical marks to insure our stressing of certain syllables. In any case, the poem's music and rhetoric cast a spell quite apart from questions of religious persuasion.

Walt Whitman, the American creator of "free verse" remains unmatched in creating a music from that form; he does not merely free himself from traditional forms, he creates new ones. "Cavalry Crossing a Ford" twice states a rhythmic motif in its first line, then builds half-line variants of that theme. Its ending opens out into two full lines of four beats each. "Bivouac on a Mountain Side" sets up a similar three-beat rhythm; here, however, variations tend to swell and include a fourth beat. Here again, the last line alters, expanding into three (rather than two) such units.

Whitman's "Tears," influenced by Tennyson's "Break, Break, Break" and "Tears, Idle Tears," establishes a three-beat motif of monosyllables. His variations, however, lengthen the whole line with more and more stress groups so that the climactic lines grow to six or eight stresses. This follows our common inclination to build sentences from a series of short phrases, each with one stressed noun or verb; thus, in the de/composition, I was able to subvert Whitman's rhythms simply by turning his language polysyllabic and pretentious.

In James Stephens's "The Main Deep," the approach and crash of a single wave is depicted in a repeated two-beat pulse that climaxes into three full beats, and by the growing intimacy of adjectives: "glacid . . . cold . . . chill." Continuous motion is further suggested by the use of gerunds and participles and by the incomplete syntax.

George Peele's "Bethsabe's Song" (from his 1599 play *The Love of King David and Fair Bethsabe*), probably intended to imitate classical meters based on syllable lengths, but actually creates a stress pattern: / /, / /, / ⌣ ⌣ / /. Its almost hypnotic repetition suggests that Bethsabe, bathing on her rooftop, is half-dazed both by the sun and by her own beauty, which she implicitly compares to it. The final lines approach a more common iambic trimeter, so contributing to her recognition of danger—King David is, even now, spying on her. In my de/composition, she becomes so conscious of her peril that it is folly to continue.

In "The Return," Ezra Pound portrays a group of men retreating in defeat; the opening lines clearly imitate their broken movements. Later, however, a rhythmic theme (derived from the opening) is announced: / ⌣ ⌣ / ⌣ / and is then varied through the rest of the poem. Pound's "In a Station of the Metro" has been described as "an atom of poetry, but a whole atom" skillfully binding a negative and a positive charge. My first two de/compositions turn the charge either all positive or all negative, so undoing the structure. Pound's poem, like Peele's, is based on a classical quantitative meter, though both use English stress as determinant. Lacking line breaks, the prose de/composition, though words and stress remain unaltered, curtails the rhythmic movement.

Marianne Moore's "No Swan so Fine" uses a syllabic meter: each stanza has seven lines whose syllable count runs 7 8 6 8 8 5 9; the second and fifth lines rhyme. Her first stanza builds to a delicious rhythm, rather like a drum riff. I have not only obliterated this but, later, weakened the contrast between the artwork's permanence and the powerful king's mortality.

"The Mind is an Enchanting Thing" is composed in six-line stanzas with the syllable count: 6 5 4 6 7 9. The first and third lines rhyme, as do the fourth and fifth. Rhyming syllables, however, may have no stress, so hiding the rhyme and allowing her to be either as prosy or as musical as she wishes. Here, she often chooses a triple rhythm but is free to break that movement at will.

Louis MacNeice's "Bagpipe Music" follows, freely, a standard form for songs or folkish poems: a half-line of four stresses followed by one of three. Lacking this form, his satire on Scottish life in the 1930s loses all crispness and sense of rowdy fun.

W. H. Auden, who experimented with many verse forms, in "Musée des Beaux Arts" takes on random rhymes and conversational language—somewhat like Ogden Nash—turning them to serious purpose. The de/composition converts this to Neoclassical "heroic" rhyming couplets with remarkably unheroic results.

In his "Song of the Old Soldier," the beginning of each stanza describes its hero's uncivil civilian life in shambling, floppy lines; the second half, portraying his Army life, is fittingly regimented and repetitive. My de/composition reverses these qualities, preserving little of Auden's provocative wit and even less of the implications of his technique—that George's lack of individual purpose or restraint makes him the pawn of whatever authorities come to control his life.

In earlier centuries, English verse lines tended to coincide with phrases or units of syntax—most notably in the eighteenth century's "heroic" couplets. William Carlos Williams often sets out, deliberately, to fracture any such correspondence; the reader is involved in the conflict between line and sense. In both "Queen-Anne's-Lace" and "Spring and All," the effort spent to establish syntax gives greater cogency and value to this meaning when recognized, simply because we've had to fight for it. In "Poem," our hesitancy in moving through the disrupted syntax delightfully imitates the hesitant and cautious movements of the exploring cat; its final step into the earthy and prosaic flowerpot jolts the whole preceding sentence into shape and closure—much as a final rhyme often did for more traditional poets.

V

Structure & Climax

London

—William Blake, 1794

I wander thro' each charter'd street,
Near where the charter'd Thames does flow,
And mark in every face I meet
Marks of weakness, marks of woe.

In every cry of every Man,
In every Infant's cry of fear,
In every voice, in every ban,
The mind-forg'd manacles I hear.

How the Chimney-sweeper's cry
Every black'ning Church appalls;
And the hapless Soldier's sigh
Runs in blood down Palace walls.

But most through midnight streets I hear
How the youthful Harlot's curse
Blasts the new-born Infant's tear,
And blights with plagues the Marriage hearse.

London

—an earlier version of Blake's last stanza

But most the midnight's Harlot's curse
From every dismal street I hear,
Weaves around the Marriage hearse
And blasts the new-born Infant's tear.

Ozymandias

—Percy Bysshe Shelley

I met a traveller from an antique land
Who said: Two vast and trunkless legs of stone
Stand in the desert . . . Near them, on the sand,
Half sunk, a shattered visage lies, whose frown,
And wrinkled lip, and sneer of cold command,
Tell that its sculptor well those passions read
Which yet survive, stamped on these lifeless things,
The hand that mocked them and the heart that fed:
And on the pedestal these words appear:
"My name is Ozymandias, king of kings:
Look on my works, ye Mighty, and despair!"
Nothing beside remains. Round the decay
Of that colossal wreck, boundless and bare
The lone and level sands stretch far away.

Ozymandias

—endings de/composed from Shelley

"My name is Ozymandias, king of kings:
Look on my works, ye Mighty, and despair
Of leaving name, face or one thought behind—
No monument, no testament or heir,
No faintest trace another age might find."

"My name is Ozymandias, king of kings:
Look on my works, ye Mighty, and rejoice:
Though Man and everything he builds must die
Given good fortune and the proper choice
You still can rule your world the same as I."

"My name is Ozymandias, king of kings:
Look on my works, ye Mighty, and admire
The splendors of my buildings and my Art.
Though death and dust shall bury each empire,
Great art alone endures to rule the heart."

Skunk Hour

(For Elizabeth Bishop)

—Robert Lowell

Nautilus Island's hermit
heiress still lives through winter in her Spartan cottage;
her sheep still graze above the sea.
Her son's a bishop. Her farmer
is first selectman in our village;
she's in her dotage.

Thirsting for
the hierarchic privacy
of Queen Victoria's century,
she buys up all
the eyesores facing her shore,
and lets them fall.

The season's ill—
we've lost our summer millionaire,
who seemed to leap from an L. L. Bean
catalogue. His nine-knot yawl
was auctioned off to lobstermen.
A red fox stain covers Blue Hill.

And now our fairy
decorator brightens his shop for fall;
His fishnet's filled with orange cork,
orange, his cobbler's bench and awl;
there is no money in his work,
he'd rather marry.

Raccoon Time

—de/composed from Lowell

Nautilus Island's penny-pinching
heiress still lives through winter in her Spartan cottage;
her sheep still graze above the sea.
Her son's a bishop. Her farmer
is first selectman in our village;
she's decrepit with old age.

Thirsting for
the hierarchic snobbery
of Queen Victoria's century,
she has to buy
all the eyesores facing her shore
to gentrify.

The season's gone chill—
we've lost our summer millionaire
who seemed to leap from an L. L. Bean
catalogue. His nine-knot yawl
was auctioned off to lobstermen.
A red fox stain covers Blue Hill.

And now our local
decorator brightens his shop for fall;
his fishnet's filled with orange cork,
orange, his cobbler's bench and awl;
there is no money in his work;
the wealthy snub him as a yokel.

Skunk Hour (continued)

One dark night,
my Tudor Ford climbed the hill's skull;
I watched for love-cars. Lights turned down,
they lay together, hull to hull,
where the graveyard shelves on the town. . . .
My mind's not right.

A car radio bleats,
"Love, O careless Love. . . ." I hear
my ill-spirit sob in each blood cell,
as if my hand were at its throat. . . .
I myself am hell;
nobody's here—

only skunks, that search
in the moonlight for a bite to eat.
They march on their soles up Main Street:
white stripes, moonstruck eyes' red fire
under the chalk-dry and spar spire
of the Trinitarian Church.

I stand on top
of our back steps and breathe the rich air—
a mother skunk with her column of kittens swills the garbage pail.
She jabs her wedge-head in a cup
of sour cream, drops her ostrich tail,
and will not scare.

One dark night,
my two-door Ford climbed the hill's skull;
I watched for love-cars. Lights turned down,
they lay together, hull to hull,
where the harbor shelves on the town. . . .
To spy on them's not right.

A car radio bleats
"Love, O careless Love. . . ." I hear
my sad spirit sob in each blood cell,
as if my hand were at its throat. . . .
To live like this is hell;
nobody else is here—

just raccoons that search
in the moonlight for a bite to eat.
They lope on their soles up Main Street;
tail stripes, moonstruck eyes' red fire
under the chalk-dry and spar spire
of the Trinitarian Church.

I stand on top
of our back steps and breathe the cool air—
a mother coon with her pack of cubs
scours our barnyard.
She scratches at the door
of our henhouse, bares her teeth
and will not scare.

Deer Evening

—alternate de/composition of final stanzas

only deer, that search
in the moonlight for a bite to eat.
They stalk on sharp hooves up Main Street:
long legs, moonstruck eyes' red fire
under the chalk-dry and spar spire
of the Trinitarian Church.

I stand on top
of our back steps and breathe the cool air—
a doe with two fauns forages our orchard.
She lifts her head, bringing up
a ripe apple, drops her warning tail,
and will not scare.

Eight O'Clock

—A. E. Housman

He stood, and heard the steeple
   Sprinkle the quarters on the morning town.
One, two, three, four, to market-place and people
   It tossed them down.

Strapped, noosed, nighing his hour,
   He stood and counted them and cursed his luck;
And then the clock collected in the tower
   Its strength, and struck.

↻ Eight A.M.

—de/composed from Housman

He stood, and heard the steeple
   Telling the hour to the village crowd
With measured voice; for market-place and people
   It rang aloud.

Nearing his final hour—
   The noose in place, arms tied—he questioned Fate;
Then, tolling his death sentence from the tower,
   The clock struck eight.

Parting, Without a Sequel

—John Crowe Ransom

She has finished and sealed the letter
At last, which he so richly has deserved,
With characters venomous and hatefully curved,
And nothing could be better.

But even as she gave it
Saying to the blue-capped functioneer of doom,
"Into his hands," she hoped the leering groom
Might somewhere lose and leave it.

Then all the blood
Forsook her face. She was too pale for tears,
Observing the ruin of her younger years.
She went and stood

Under her father's vaunting oak
Who kept his peace in wind and sun, and glistened
Stoical in the rain; to whom she listened
If he spoke.

And now the agitation of the rain
Rasped his sere leaves, and he talked low and gentle
Reproaching the wan daughter by the lintel;
Ceasing and beginning again.

Away went the messenger's bicycle,
His serpent's track went up the hill forever,
And all the time she stood there hot as fever
And cold as any icicle.

Parting Forever

—de/composed from Ransom

At last she has signed and sealed the letter
Which by bad misbehavior he had earned,
In which her anger and resentment burned
And this makes her feel better.

But even as she gave it,
Telling the messenger in his cap of blue,
"Deliver this in person," she hoped, too,
The boy would lose and leave it.

Then all the blood
Drained from her cheeks. She felt too faint to weep,
Knowing the loss she'd suffered was so deep.
She went and stood

Under a neighbor's great, strong oak
That kept quiet through wind and sun and gleamed
Wet in the rain. She listened till it seemed
To her he spoke.

And now the soft pattering of the rain
Shook its dry leaves; it murmured soft and low
To comfort the young woman there below
Soothing her again.

The messenger went up the hill,
His twisting track seemed to go on forever;
Meanwhile, she stood there hot as any fever
But also in a chill.

I Never Lost As Much But Twice

—Emily Dickinson

I never lost as much but twice,
And that was in the sod.
Twice have I stood a beggar
Before the door of God!

Angels—twice descending
Reimbursed my store—
Burglar! Banker—Father!
I am poor once more!

↻ I've Lost So Much

—de/composed from Dickinson

I've lost so much just twice before—
When loved ones passed to sod.
Twice have I stood a beggar
Before the throne of God.

Angels—twice descending
Reimbursed my store—
Sweet and gentle Father,
I need your help once more.

This Be The Verse

—Philip Larkin

They fuck you up, your mum and dad.
    They may not mean to, but they do.
They fill you with the faults they had
    And add some extra, just for you.

But they were fucked up in their turn
    By fools in old-style hats and coats,
Who half the time were soppy-stern
    And half at one another's throats.

Man hands on misery to man.
    It deepens like a coastal shelf.
Get out as early as you can,
    And don't have any kids yourself.

The Essential Verse

—de/composed from Larkin

They spoil your life, your parents do
    Though that may not be what they meant.
They pass their own faults on to you
    With new neuroses they'll invent.

But they were messed up equally
    By customs of an earlier age—
Strict rules, sentimentality,
    Which filled them with enduring rage.

We give each other pain and strife
    That spread through all man's universe.
Don't foolishly extend your life
    And raising children would be worse.

Whoso List to Hunt

—Sir Thomas Wyatt

Whoso list[1] to hunt, I know where is an hind,[2]
    But as for me, alas, I may no more;
    The vain travail hath wearied me so sore,
    I am of them that furthest cometh behind.
Yet may I by no means my wearied mind
    Draw from the deer, but as she fleeth afore
    Fainting I follow; I leave off therefore,
    Since in a net I seek to hold the wind.
Who list her hunt, I put him out of doubt,
    As well as I, may spend his time in vain.
    And graven with diamonds in letters plain,
There is written her fair neck round about,
    "*Noli me tangere,*[3] for Caesar's I am,
    And wild for to hold, though I seem tame."

---

[1]Whoever likes.
[2]Female red deer.
[3]Do not touch me.

Whoso List to Hunt

—de/composition of Wyatt's sestet

Who list her hunt may spend his time in vain
As well as I, I put him out of doubt
And there is graven with diamonds round about
The neck of that fair dear in letters plain
    Never to touch her for she is the king's
    And wild to hold beyond all living things.

Holy Sonnet #7

—John Donne

At the round earth's imagined corners, blow
Your trumpets, angels, and arise, arise
From death, you numberless infinities
Of souls, and to your scattered bodies go;
All whom the flood did, and fire shall, o'erthrow,
All whom war, dearth, age, agues, tyrannies,
Despair, law, chance, hath slain, and you whose eyes
Shall behold God, and never taste death's woe.
But let them sleep, Lord, and me mourn a space;
For, if above all these, my sins abound,
'Tis late to ask abundance of Thy grace
When we are there. Here on this lowly ground,
Teach me how to repent; for that's as good
As if Thou hadst sealed my pardon with Thy blood.

Wholly Undonne

—de/composed from Donne

At earth's imagined compass points and poles,
Now all you angels, let your trumpets blow
Then rise from death, you multitudes of souls
And to your scattered bodies swiftly go:
All whom the deluge or whom fire did kill,
Whom war or dearth, disease or age has slain,
Laws, tyrants, accidents; those living still
Who'll see the Lord yet need not feel death's pain.
But wait, Lord; let them sleep on while I grieve
For if my sins are more than all of these
'Tis late to ask forgiveness and reprieve
On Judgement Day. Here, bending on my knees,
I do implore instruction in repentance
Which dost insure that Thou'lt commute my sentence.

To Autumn

—John Keats

I

Season of mists and mellow fruitfulness,
    Close bosom-friend of the maturing sun;
Conspiring with him how to load and bless
    With fruit the vines that round the thatch-eves run;
To bend with apples the mossed cottage-trees,
    And fill all fruit with ripeness to the core;
        To swell the gourd, and plump the hazel shells
    With a sweet kernel; to set budding more,
And still more, later flowers for the bees,
Until they think warm days will never cease,
        For Summer has o'er-brimmed their clammy cells.

II

Who hath not seen thee oft amid thy store?
    Sometimes whoever seeks abroad may find
Thee sitting careless on a granary floor,
    Thy hair soft-lifted by the winnowing wind;
Or on a half-reaped furrow sound asleep,
    Drowsed with the fume of poppies, while thy hook
        Spares the next swath and all its twinéd flowers:
And sometimes like a gleaner thou dost keep
    Steady thy laden head across a brook;
    Or by a cider-press, with patient look,
        Thou watchest the last oozings hours by hours.

↻ To Autumn

—de/composed passages from Keats in italics

I

Season of mists and mellow fruitfulness,
    Close bosom-friend of the maturing sun;
Conspiring with him how to load and bless
    With fruit the vines that round the thatch-eves run;
To bend with apples the mossed cottage-trees,
    And fill all fruit with ripeness to the core;
        To swell the gourd, and plump the hazel shells
    With a sweet kernel; to set budding more,
And still more, later flowers for the bees,
Until they think warm days will never cease,
    For summer's nectar has o'er-brimmed their cells.

II

Who hath not seen thee oft amid thy store?
    Sometimes whoever seeks abroad may find
Thee sitting careless on a granary floor,
    Thy hair soft-lifted by the winnowing wind;
Or on a half-reaped furrow sound asleep,
    Drowsed with the *poppies' fumes—thy bare arm's crook*
        Curled 'round the next swath and its twinéd flowers:
And sometimes like a gleaner thou dost keep
    Steady thy laden head across a brook;
    Or by a cider-press, with patient look,
        Thou watchest *the rich droplets* hours by hours.

To Autumn (continued)

III

Where are the songs of Spring? Aye, where are they?
    Think not of them, thou hast thy music too—
While barréd clouds bloom the soft-dying day,
    And touch the stubble-plains with rosy hue;
Then in a wailful choir the small gnats mourn
    Among the river sallows, borne aloft
        Or sinking as the light wind lives or dies;
And full-grown lambs loud bleat from hilly bourn;
    Hedge crickets sing; and now with treble soft
    The redbreast whistles from a garden-croft;
        And gathering swallows twitter in the skies.

To Autumn (continued)

III

Who cares for songs of Spring? What use are they?
    You have your music and your beauties too—
While clouds are dyed by the sun's crimson ray
    Touching the meadows with a rosy hue;
Then in a clustering swarm the small gnats ride
    Among the river willows, borne aloft
        And fluttering when the evening breezes rise.
Now full-grown sheep graze on the near hillside;
    The fireflies spark; and now alighting soft
    The redbreast settles on a garden-croft
        And flocks of swallows fly home through the skies.

Loveliest of Trees

—A. E. Housman

Loveliest of trees, the cherry now
Is hung with bloom along the bough,
And stands about the woodland ride
Wearing white for Eastertide.

Now, of my threescore years and ten,
Twenty will not come again,
And take from seventy springs a score,
It only leaves me fifty more.

And since to look at things in bloom
Fifty springs are little room,
About the woodlands I will go
To see the cherry hung with snow.

↻ Loveliest of Trees

 —de/composed from Housman

Loveliest of trees, the cherry now
Is hung with bloom along the bough
And stands about the forest side
Trimmed with white for Eastertide.

Now, of my threescore years and ten,
Twenty will not come again
And, take from seventy years a score,
I should have all of fifty more.

And since to look at things in bloom,
Fifty years leaves lots of room,
I'll take time from life's harried race
To see these cherries strung with lace.

The Fish

—Elizabeth Bishop

I caught a tremendous fish
and held him beside the boat
half out of water, with my hook
fast in corner of his mouth.
He didn't fight.
He hadn't fought at all.
He hung a grunting weight,
battered and venerable
and homely. Here and there
his brown skin hung in strips
like ancient wallpaper,
and its pattern of darker brown
was like wallpaper:
shapes like full-blown roses
stained and lost through age.
He was speckled with barnacles,
fine rosettes of lime,
and infested
with tiny white sea-lice,
and underneath two or three
rags of green weed hung down.
While his gills were breathing in
the terrible oxygen
—the frightening gills,
fresh and crisp with blood,
that can cut so badly—
I thought of the coarse white flesh
packed in like feathers,
the big bones and the little bones,

A Huge Fish

—de/composed passages from Bishop in italics

I caught a *huge* fish
and held him beside the boat
half out of water, *though the lure*
was still held in his mouth.
He didn't *thrash around.*
He hadn't *thrashed around* at all.
He hung a *hefty* weight,
battered and *dilapidated*
and homely. Here and there
his brown skin hung in strips
like *old* wallpaper,
and its pattern of darker brown
was like wallpaper:
shapes like *rectangles and circles*
stained and *faded* with time.
He was *spotted* with barnacles,
small *abscesses* of lime,
and *full*
of tiny white sea-lice,
and underneath two or three
rags of green weed hung down.
While his gills were *letting in*
the *unfamiliar* oxygen
—the *strange* gills,
striped and *marked* with blood,
whose loss is so weakening—
I thought of the coarse white *meat*
packed in like feathers,
the big bones and the little bones,

The Fish (continued)

the dramatic reds and blacks
of his shiny entrails,
and the pink swim-bladder
like a big peony.
I looked into his eyes
which were far larger than mine
but shallower, and yellowed,
the irises backed and packed
with tarnished tinfoil
seen through the lenses
of old scratched isinglass.
They shifted a little, but not
to return my stare.
—It was more like the tipping
of an object toward the light.
I admired his sullen face,
the mechanism of his jaw,
and then I saw
that from his lower lip
—if you could call it a lip—
grim, wet, and weaponlike,
hung five old pieces of fish-line,
or four and a wire leader
with the swivel still attached,
with all their five big hooks
grown firmly in his mouth.
A green line, frayed at the end
where he broke it, two heavier lines,
and a fine black thread
still crimped from the strain and snap

the *garish* reds and blacks
of his *slippery* entrails,
and the *purple* swim-bladder
like a big *puffball*.
I *noticed that* his eyes
were far larger than mine
but shallower, and yellowed,
the irises backed and packed
with tarnished tinfoil
seen through the *layers*
of old scratched isinglass.
They shifted a little, but not
to *turn my way*.
—It was more like the tipping
of an object *to a different angle*.
I *scrutinized* his sullen face,
the mechanism of his jaw,
and then I saw
that from his lower lip
—if you could call *that thing* a lip—
grim, wet and weaponlike,
hung five old pieces of fish-line,
or four and a *nylon* leader
with the *bobber* still attached,
with all their five big hooks
grown firmly in his mouth.
A green line, frayed at the end
where *it had broken*, two heavier lines,
and a fine black thread
still crimped from the strain and snap

when it broke and he got away.
Like medals with their ribbons
frayed and wavering,
a five-haired beard of wisdom
trailing from his aching jaw.
I stared and stared
and victory filled up
the little rented boat,
from the pool of bilge
where oil had spread a rainbow
around the rusted engine
to the bailer rusted orange,
the sun-cracked thwarts,
the oarlocks on their strings,
the gunnels—until everything
was rainbow, rainbow, rainbow!
And I let the fish go.

when it broke and *somebody lost him*.
Like the ends of *kite strings or kitetails*
frayed and wavering,
a five-haired *fringe of experience*
trailing from his *bulging* jaw.
I stared and stared
and *my triumph* filled up
the little rented boat,
from the pool of bilge
where oil had spread a *varicolored film*
around the rusted engine
to the bailer rusted orange,
the *cracked and weathered* thwarts,
the oarlocks on their strings,
the gunnels—until everything
was *victory, victory, victory!*
And I *tossed* the fish *away*.

She Dwelt Among the Untrodden Ways

—William Wordsworth

She dwelt among the untrodden[1] ways
    Beside the springs of Dove,
A Maid whom there were none to praise
    And very few to love:

A violet by a mossy stone
    Half hidden from the eye!
—Fair as a star, when only one
    Is shining in the sky.

She lived unknown, and few could know
    When Lucy ceased to be;
But she is in her grave, and, oh,
    The difference to me!

---

[1]Not only "untrampled" but also suggestive of purity; "tread" was the common verb for the sex act of birds.

She Lived Among the Untravelled Ways

—de/composed from Wordsworth

She lived among the untravelled ways
    That high hills rise above,
A Maid whom any girl might praise
    And any man would love:

Fair as a rose beside a stone
    Half hidden from the eye!
The fairest star that anyone
    Could see in all the sky.

She dwelt unheard of, few could know
    That she was dead, but she
Is sleeping her last sleep, and oh,
    How great a loss to me!

She Dwelt Among the Untrodden Ways

—Wordsworth, first version

My hope was one, from cities far,
    Nursed on a lonesome heath;
Her lips were red as roses are,
    Her hair a woodbine wreath.

She dwelt among the untrodden ways
    Beside the springs of Dove.
A Maid whom there were none to praise
    And very few to love;

A violet by a mossy stone
    Half hidden from the eye!
—Fair as a star, when only one
    Is shining in the sky.

And she was graceful as the broom
    That flowers by Carron's side;
But slow distemper checked her bloom
    And on the heath she died.

Long time before her head lay low
    Dead to the world was she;
But now she's in her grave, and oh,
    The difference to me!

A Slumber Did My Spirit Seal

—William Wordsworth

A slumber did my spirit seal;
    I had no human fears:
She seemed a thing that could not feel
    The touch of earthly years.

No motion has she now, no force;
    She neither hears nor sees;
Rolled round in earth's diurnal course,
    With rocks, and stones, and trees.

↻ A Slumber Did My Poem Steal

—de/composed from Wordsworth

My soul slept soundly all that time;
    I hadn't any fears:
She seemed a person too sublime
    For death to end her years.

But she is dead so I've been forced
    To come alive and see
She, too, endures earth's daily course,
    The same as you and me.

Bells for John Whiteside's Daughter

—John Crowe Ransom

There was such speed in her little body,
And such lightness in her footfall,
It is no wonder her brown study
Astonishes us all.

Her wars were bruited in our high window.
We looked among orchard trees and beyond
Where she took arms against her shadow,
Or harried unto the pond

The lazy geese, like a snow cloud
Dripping their snow on the green grass,
Tricking and stopping, sleepy and proud,
Who cried in goose, Alas,

For the tireless heart within the little
Lady with rod that made them rise
From their noon apple-dreams and scuttle
Goose-fashion under the skies!

But now go the bells, and we are ready,
In one house we are sternly stopped
To say we are vexed at her brown study,
Lying so primly propped.

A Little Girl's Funeral

—de/composed from Ransom

There was such life in her compact frame,
And such zest in how swift she'd run,
Her sudden grim mood seems a shame,
Saddening everyone.

We gossiped about her toils and throes
Or watched where, through the orchard trees,
She fought imaginary foes
Or chased the lazy geese

Down to the pond like a wintry cloud
Shedding loose feathers white as snow,
Waddling stiffly, slow and proud,
Squawking in goose-talk, "Oh!"

Because the naughty, mischievous heart
And the stick that little girl would wield
Would wake them from sweet dreams to start
Scuttling across the field.

But now the bells toll, rousing us
From this house where we sadly wait
To say we're saddened by her serious
Mood and tragic fate.

England in 1819

—Percy Bysshe Shelley

An old, mad, blind, despised and dying king;
Princes, the dregs of their dull race, who flow
Through public scorn—mud from a muddy spring;
Rulers, who neither see, nor feel, nor know,
But leech-like to their fainting country cling,
Till they drop, blind in blood, without a blow;
A people starved and stabbed in the untilled field;
An army which liberticide and prey
Makes as a two-edged sword to all who wield;
Golden and sanguine laws which tempt and slay;
Religion Christless, Godless—a book sealed;
A Senate—Time's worst statute unrepealed,
Are graves from which a glorious Phantom may
Burst to illumine our tempestuous day.

England in 1819

—de/composed lines from Shelley in italics

An old, mad, blind, despised and dying king,
Princes, the dregs of their dull race, who flow
Through public scorn—mud from a muddy spring;
Rulers, who neither see, nor feel, nor know,
But leech-like to their fainting country cling,
Till they drop, blind in blood, without a blow;
A people starved and stabbed in the untilled field;
An army which liberticide and prey
Makes as a two-edged sword to all who wield;
Golden and sanguine laws which tempt and slay;
Religion Christless, Godless—a book sealed;
A Senate—Time's worst statute unrepealed,
Show a society in deep decay
That's lost all hope of finding its true way.

Richard Cory

—Edwin Arlington Robinson

Whenever Richard Cory went down town,
We people on the pavement looked at him:
He was a gentleman from sole to crown,
Clean favored, and imperially slim.

And he was always quietly arrayed,
And he was always human when he talked;
But still he fluttered pulses when he said,
"Good morning," and he glittered when he walked.

And he was rich—yes, richer than a king—
And admirably schooled in every grace:
In fine, we thought that he was everything
To make us wish that we were in his place.

So on we worked, and waited for the light,
And went without the meat, and cursed the bread;
And Richard Cory, one calm summer night,
Went home and put a bullet through his head.

↻ Richer Quarry

—de/composed from Robinson

Wherever Richard Cory chanced to go
The people he encountered looked at him:
He was a gentleman from top to toe,
Good-looking, in the height of style and slim.

He always dressed in tasteful hats and suits
And he was always friendly when he talked;
But hearts beat faster after his salutes,
"Hello, there!" or to see the way he walked.

He was so rich—yes, richer than a king—
And had an inborn sense of charm and grace:
In short, we thought that he had everything
And we should feel he filled an envied place.

So on we labored without heat or light,
Had rotten food so some grew sick or died;
While Richard Cory, one hot autumn night,
Amazed us by committing suicide.

The Evening Darkens Over

—Robert Bridges

The evening darkens over.
After a day so bright
The windcapt waves discover
That wild will be the night.
There's sound of distant thunder.

The latest sea-birds hover
Along the cliff's sheer height;
As in the memory wander
Last flutterings of delight,
White wings lost on the white.

There's not a ship in sight;
And as the sun goes under
Thick clouds conspire to cover
The moon that should rise yonder.
Thou art alone, fond lover.

Weather Report

—de/composed from Bridges

The evening darkens over.
After a day so bright
The windcapt waves discover
There'll be a storm tonight.
There's sound of distant thunder.

The latest sea-birds wander
Along the cliff's sheer height;
As a great hawk or condor
Might sweep across one's sight,
Dark wings against the white.

There's not a ship in sight;
The sun's gone down. I wonder
If thick clouds will soon cover
The moon that's shining yonder.
We must go in, fond lover.

Seen When Nights Are Silent

—W. H. Auden

Seen when nights are silent,
The bean-shaped island
And our ugly comic servant,
Who was observant.

O the veranda and the fruit,
The tiny steamer in the bay
Startling summer with its hoot:—
You have gone away.

Seen When Night Is Soundless

—de/composed from Auden

Seen when night is soundless,
The island dark and boundless,
And our servant, droll and dumpy,
Who kept us comfy.

O the veranda and the flowers,
The little steamer's throaty call
Telling the harbor town the hours:—
Come; enjoy it all.

Sir Patrick Spens

—Scottish Folk Ballad

The king sits in Dumferling toune,
    Drinking the blude-reid wine:
"O whar will I get me a skeely sailor,   *skillful*
    To sail this schip of mine?"

Up and spak an eldern knicht,   *elderly knight*
    Sat at the king's richt kne: *right knee*
"Sir Patrick Spens is the best sailor
    That sails upon the se."

The king has written a braid letter,   *broad; forthright*
    And signd it wi his hand,
And sent it to Sir Patrick Spens,
    Was walking on the strand.

The first line that Sir Patrick red,
    A loud lauch lauched he;   *laugh*
The next line that Sir Patrick red,
    The teir blinded his ee.   *tear . . . eye*

"O wha is this has done this deid,
    This ill deid don to me,
To send me out this time o' the yeir,
    To sail upon the se!

"Mak haste, mak haste, my mirry men all,
    Our guid schip sails the morne":
"O say na sae, my master deir,   *not so*
    For I feir a deadlie storme."

Sir Patrick Spens

—de/composed from the Scottish ballad

The king sits in a coastal town
    Drinking the dark red wine:
"O where will I get a good sailor,
    To sail this ship of mine?"

Up and spake a pert, young knight,
    Sat at the king's right hand:
"Sir Patrick Spens is the best sailor,
    In Scotland's rocky land."

The king has written a broad letter,
    Signed it with his own hand,
And sent it to Sir Patrick Spens,
    Who was travelling through the land.

The first line that Sir Patrick read,
    His heart was filled with glee;
The next line that Sir Patrick read,
    A sadder man was he.

"O who has done this wicked deed,
    This deed of foul betrayal,
To send me out this time o' the year,
    Upon the sea to sail?"

Yet still he bade his sailors all
    Make ready to embark
Though when his orders came to them,
    They saw their hopes grow dark.

Sir Patrick Spens (continued)

"Late, late yestreen I saw the new moone,   *last night*
  Wi the auld moone in hir arme,
And I feir, I feir, my master deir,
  That we will cum to harme."

O our Scots nobles wer richt laith   *very loath*
  To weet their cork-heild schoone;   *shoes*
Bot lang owre a' the play wer played   *long before*
  Thair hats they swam aboone,   *about*

O, it's mony and mony a feather-bed
  Went fluchterin' to the faim   *fluttering . . . foam*
And mony and mony a Scot lord's son
  Will never mair cum hame.   *home*

O lang, lang may their ladies sit,
  Wi thair fans into thair hand,
Or eir they se Sir Patrick Spens
  Cum sailing to the land.

O lang, lang may the ladies stand,
  Wi thair gold kems in thair hair,   *combs*
Waiting for thair ain deir lords,
  For they'll se thame na mair.

Haf owre, haf owre to Aberdour,   *Halfway across*
  It's fiftie fadom deip,
And thair lies guid Sir Patrick Spens,
  Wi the Scots lords at his feit.

"Last night I saw the new moon curled
    'Round the fading older moon;
And I'm very sure, my master dear,
    We'll have foul weather soon."

To see wet brine on their high-heeled shoes,
    Filled our Scots lairds with loathing,
But long ere all the play was played
    They swam in all their clothing.

O, it's many and many a stout seachest
    Was sunk beneath the foam
And many and many of Scotland's best
    Will never more come home.

O a long time may their ladies sit,
    With their prayerbooks in their hand,
Before they'll see Sir Patrick Spens
    Come sailing to the land.

O it's longer yet may the ladies stand,
    With black bands in their hair,
Waiting for their own dear lairds,
    But they'll see them na mair.

Halfway across to Aberdour,
    It's fifty fathoms down,
And there lies good Sir Patrick Spens,
    With the Scot lairds all around.

Edward

"Why does your brand sae drap wi' bluid,   *sword / so*
        Edward, Edward,
Why does your brand sae drap wi' bluid,
        And why sae sad gang ye, O?"   *go*
"O, I ha'e killed my hawk sae guid
        Mither, mither,
O, I ha'e killed my hawk sae guid,
        And I had nae mair but he, O!"

"Your hawke's bluid was never sae reid,   *red*
        Edward, Edward,
Your hawke's bluid was never sae reid,
        My dear son I tell thee, O."
"O, I ha'e killed my reid-roan steed,
        Mither, mither,
O, I ha'e killed my reid-roan steed,
        That erst was sae fair and free, O."

"Your steed was auld, and ye ha'e gat mair;
        Edward, Edward,
Your steed was auld, and ye ha'e gat mair,
        Some other dule ye dree, O."   *grief / suffer*
"O, I ha'e killed my ain fader dear,
        Mither, mither,
O, I ha'e killed my ain fader dear,
        Alas, and wae is me, O!"   *woe*

"And whatten penance wul ye dree for that,   *what sort of*
        Edward, Edward?

The Bad Son

—de/composed from the Ballad of Edward

Why dois your brand sae drap wi' bluid,
    Edward, Edward;
Why dois your brand sae drap wi' bluid,
    And why sae sad gang ye, O?
"O, I hae killed my hawk sae guid
    Mither, Mither,
O, I hae killed my hawk sae guid
    And I had nae mair but he, O!"

You've many a hawk so swift and sound,
    Edward, Edward,
You've many a hawk so swift and sound,
    My deir son, I tell thee, O!
"O, I hae killed my milk-white hound,
    Mither, Mither,
O, I hae killed my milk-white hound,
    That tracked fresh game for me, O!"

Your white hound lagged in the chase's rear,
    Edward, Edward,
Your white hound lagged in the chase's rear;
    Some other dule ye dree, O!
"O, I hae killed my ain fadir deir,
    Mither, Mither,
O, I hae killed my ain fadir deir;
    Alas and wae is me, O!"

Alack, how shall we hide this guilt,
    Edward, Edward,

Edward (continued)

And whatten penance wul ye dree for that,
    My dear son, now tell me, O?"
"I'll set my feet in yonder boat,
    Mither, mither,
I'll set my feet in yonder boat,
    And I'll gang over the sea, O."

"And what wul ye do wi' your towers and your ha',
    Edward, Edward?
And what wul ye do wi' your towers and your ha',
    That were sae fair to see, O?"
"I'll let them stand tul they down fa',
    Mither, mither,
"I'll let them stand tul they down fa',
    For here never mair maun I be, O."   *must*

"And what wul ye leave to your bairns and your wife,   *children*
    Edward, Edward?
And what wul ye leave to your bairns and your wife,
    Whan ye gang over the sea, O?"
"The warlde's room, let them beg thrae life,   *through*
    Mither, mither,
The warlde's room, let them beg thrae life,
    For them never mair wul I see, O."

"And what wul ye leave to your ain mither dear,
    Edward, Edward?
And what wul ye leave to your ain mither dear,
    My dear son, now tell me, O?"

The Bad Son (continued)

Alack, how shall we hide this guilt
    Sae dangerous to thee, O?
"To the king I'll own what bluid I've spilt,
    Mither, Mither,
To the king I'll own what bluid I've spilt
    Upon my bended knee, O!"

And what will you do for your bairns and your wife,
    Edward, Edward,
What will you do for your bairns and your wife,
    That weak and helpless be, O?
"O, the king and court must ordain their life
    Mither, Mither,
The king and court must ordain their life
    If I may not gang free, O!"

And what will ye do wi' your towers and your ha',
    Edward, Edward,
What will ye do wi' your towers and your ha'
    Should they judge ill o' thee, O?
"O, the king must now dispose of all,
    Mither, Mither,
The king must now dispose of all
    If he'll nae pardon gie, O!"

And what will ye leave to your ain mither deir,
    Edward, Edward,
What will ye leave to your ain mither deir,
    My deir son, now tell me, O?

Edward (continued)

"The curse of hell frae me sall ye bear,   *from / shall*
    Mither, mither,
The curse of hell frae me sall ye bear,
    Sic counsels ye gave to me, O."   *such*

The Bad Son (continued)

"A sad and sorrowful widow's tear,
    Mither, Mither,
A sad and sorrowful widow's tear
    And all on account of me, O!"

V. Structure & Climax

Those poems we have long valued and preserved have usually been the ones in which the whole IS more than the sum of the parts. Words, phrases, sentences are enriched by comparison and contrast with each other and with other elements of the poem, so building a structure that culminates in a peak of insight or emotion. This structure is the poem's real form, far more significant than shaping patterns like the sonnet, couplet, villanelle, etc.—though these may influence and assist the process of meaning and feeling. Something similar is true, of course, for any art form taking place in time—music, drama, fiction, dance—or, as far as that goes, for direct conflicts like boxing. Having landed your best punch, you hope to stride rapidly from the arena.

This climax, of course, often holds the strongest statement of fact or opinion, as in "London," where, when revising, William Blake moved his "Marriage hearse" to the crucial last line, so redoubling the imagery of pestilence and disease. Percy Bysshe Shelley's "Ozymandias" reaches a peak of desolation in the ironically ambiguous epitaph, "Look on my works, ye Mighty, and despair!" The comparatively empty lines that follow dramatize, both by subject and style, the devastation of the empire. Robert Lowell's "Skunk Hour" forgoes the supercharged language and (except for one quote from Milton's Satan in line 35) the religious and literary references of his earlier "The Drunken Fisherman." Here, instead, he builds a climax from comparisons implied between its various characters and creatures; despite the elaborate stanza forms, the loss of these linkages dissolves any sense of progression.

In A.E. Housman's "Eight O'Clock," technical effects of sound and meter give reality to the execution of its subject, perhaps a petty thief. Such technical factors as the virtuoso rhyming of John Crowe Ransom's "Parting, Without a Sequel" may lend a sense of definition and closure. Elsewhere, a climactic change may be signaled by a turn in language quality: Emily Dickinson's change from humility to audacity and back again in "I Never Lost As Much But Twice"; or the switch in Philip Larkin's "This Be The Verse" from sour vulgarity to a profound, almost awestruck awareness of what harm we ignorantly do to those we love. Sir Thomas Wyatt's "Whoso List to Hunt" builds toward its climax in broken fragments of phrase (much as Housman's poem above did), importing not only a foreign language but the words of Jesus when newly risen. The deer/woman is too profane to touch and simultaneously too holy.

Poems even more frequently build to a climax by means of conflicting attitudes. The octave (first eight lines) of John Donne's "Holy Sonnet #7" calling for God's Last Judgement, is filled with violent activity and emotion, represented partly by the broken syntax and conflicting line endings, the repetition of rhyme sounds (abbaabba), and the frequent use of verbs for rhymes. The sestet (last six lines), considering the speaker's guilt and unreadiness, demands a quieter, more resigned tone.

The first two stanzas of John Keats's ode "To Autumn," focusing on pleasant aspects of the season, yield only a few hints of oncoming cold and death; the third stanza, however, (where sight seems weaker and sounds predominate), is laden with ominous suggestions. Again, in A.E. Housman's "Loveliest of Trees," the cherry blossoms first seem like Easter finery but later appear as snow, anticipating winter and death. In Elizabeth Bishop's "The Fish," we witness an open and ongoing struggle between disgust and admiration before the speaker finally yields to something like veneration.

William Wordsworth's "She Dwelt Among the Untrodden Ways" develops steadily from euphemisms and "poetic" diction toward straightforward, direct language, while its imagery simultaneously moves from suggestions of purity, innocence, and light toward darker realities. Both tendencies climax in the pivotal word "grave" as the speaker gradually manages to utter the disastrous fact. "A Slumber Did My Spirit Seal," part of the same elegaic cycle and constructed as brilliantly, mounts to the paradox that life and consciousness must spring up in a world of insensate, dumb objects, a world of "things."

The critic Yvor Winters once complained against John Crowe Ransom's

"Bells for John Whiteside's Daughter" that "the geese run away with the poem." That's exactly the point, though: the mind tries to flee the reality before it—even as the once naughty girl had chased after the geese—but it, too, is "stopped," called back by the funereal bells.

At a work's climax, not only actions, but even more often, opinions change; our attitudes often enough conceal opposites that are likely to resurface as we reconsider or learn more about our position. We find such climactic surprises in the suddenly resurrected hope in Shelley's "England in 1819" and in the hidden envy and malice of Edward Arlington Robinson's "Richard Cory." The speaker of W. H. Auden's "Seen When Nights Are Silent" does not acknowledge, perhaps has not admitted, his sense of loss till the last line. Similarly, in Robert Bridges's "The Evening Darkens Over," the ending completely changes our sense of why the speaker sees the things he mentions.

Although they tend to be highly visual, poems are concerned not merely with what we see but with how this expresses our emotions and symbolized values. Thus a development of imagery often implies a change of values—as we've already seen in several instances (e.g., "Ozymandias," "Loveliest of Trees," or "To Autumn"). The anonymous ballad "Sir Patrick Spens" reaches a climactic change of tone only by turning from the scorned Scottish nobles to the steadfast Sir Patrick. We first saw the king as larger (because more powerful) than the knights at his knee; at the end, Sir Patrick has taken the superior position, "with the Scots lairds at his feet."

Even more dramatic, often, is the contrast between the appearance of a character and the recognition of his or her real feelings and actions. A remarkable example is found in the anonymous Scottish folk ballad "Edward" where the characters' true qualities are revealed only in the last line—sending us back to re-evaluate them and all they've previously said. We have witnessed their whole scene together with no idea of the struggle going on—intimating that art, just as Aristotle said, imitates life.

Afterword

A friend of mine, a very active trial lawyer, once told me that if, in the course of an actual court case, he should need to know which witness is telling the truth and which is lying, he simply closes his eyes. People have learned, he says, to look honest, confident, and sincere; they have not learned to disguise the quality of their voices. I propose that we listen to poems with a similar ear for the genuine—much like what Quakers listen for in their silent meetings. If one member should be moved to speak, it is to testify to an "inner light" so personal that only this speaker could be "witness" to it—yet which, once spoken, is proposed as universal.

We know, though, that a poem may tell us of facts and events that never happened, perhaps never *could* happen. Can such "false testimony" confide any real news about our world and our experience? Is this "news" news, or does it fritter away our time and attention on what we've heard already? Is the witness so partisan as to be blindered against contrary evidence? Are we convinced that the witness's views are either derived from, or presented as, relevant facts and events?

Above all, does the witness, in the qualities of his or her voice, reveal anything essential about their own psyche? Does the music and movement of that voice take us into those areas of mind which often lie hidden beneath that shallow earnestness we all pretend to? Do we detect those qualities of thought and feeling which—whether we're proud of them or not—identify, more surely than any DNA sample, that incredible gift and burden: a unique human brain. Like it or not, the thoughts and feelings (i.e., the unique human brains) of those around us are the chief determinants for most of our lives; our best resource still lies in the sharing of true testimony. By the same token, whatever misrepresents the psyche leaves us poorer, less fit to decide, less able to nourish and mature our own sensibilities.

Acknowledgments

Without Donald Hall's insight and provocation,
I would not have begun this collection.

Without the lady to whom this book is dedicated,
I might find little reason to finish it.

Index of Poets

Index of Works

William De Witt Snodgrass was born in Wilkinsburg, Pennsylvania, in 1926. He has taught at universities throughout the country and has served as Distinguished Professor of Creative Writing at the University of Delaware. His more than twenty books of poetry include *The Fuehrer Bunker: The Complete Cycle* (1995); *Each in His Season* (1993); *The Fuehrer Bunker: A Cycle of Poems-in-Progress* (1977), which was nominated for the National Book Critics Circle Award for Poetry and produced by Wynn Handman for The American Place Theatre; *After Experience* (1968); and *Heart's Needle* (1959), which won the Pulitzer Prize for Poetry. Snodgrass has also produced a book of literary criticism entitled *In Radical Pursuit* (1975), and six volumes of translations, including *Selected Translations* (BOA Editions, 1998), which won the Harold Morton Landon Translation Award. His honors include an Ingram Merrill Foundation award and a special citation from the Poetry Society of America, and fellowships from The Academy of American Poets, the Ford Foundation, the Guggenheim Foundation, the National Institute of Arts and Letters, and the National Endowment for the Arts. He lives in upstate New York.

De/Compositions has been produced for Graywolf Press at Stanton Publication Services, Inc., in Saint Paul, Minnesota. The typeface, both serif and sans serif, is Legacy, designed by Ron Arnholm. Legacy reinterprets Renaissance masterpieces for digital composition. The roman is based on a type cut in Venice by Nicolas Jenson around 1469. The italic is based on letters cut in Paris by Claude Garamond around 1539. This book was designed by Wendy Holdman and has been printed on acid-free paper by Maple Vail Book Manufacturing.

Graywolf Press is a not-for-profit, independent press. The books we publish include poetry, literary fiction, essays, and cultural criticism. We are less interested in best-sellers than in talented writers who display a freshness of voice coupled with a distinct vision. We believe these are the very qualities essential to shape a vital and diverse culture.

Thankfully, many of our readers feel the same way. They have shown this through their desire to buy books by Graywolf writers; they have told us this themselves through their e-mail notes and at author events; and they have reinforced their commitment by contributing financial support, in small amounts and in large amounts, and joining the "Friends of Graywolf."

If you enjoyed this book and wish to learn more about Graywolf Press, we invite you to ask your bookseller or librarian about further Graywolf titles; or to contact us for a free catalog; or to visit our award-winning web site that features information about our forthcoming books.

We would also like to invite you to consider joining the hundreds of individuals who are already "Friends of Graywolf" by contributing to our membership program. Individual donations of any size are significant to us: they tell us that you believe that the kind of publishing we do matters. Our web site gives you many more details about the benefits you will enjoy as a "Friend of Graywolf"; but if you do not have online access, we urge you to contact us for a copy of our membership brochure.

www.graywolfpress.org

Graywolf Press
2402 University Avenue, Suite 203
Saint Paul, MN 55114
Phone: (651) 641-0077
Fax: (651) 641-0036
E-mail: wolves@graywolfpress.org